NEXT LEVEL GRAMMAR FOR A DIGITAL AGE

Co-published by Routledge and The National Council of Teachers of English

This innovative book explores how digital language and tools can be used to teach applied grammar in the classroom. With a spotlight on internet language, Crovitz, Devereaux, and Moran demonstrate how students can practice rhetorical grammar with digital tools in order to use language purposefully. With an abundance of original strategies, prompts, and questions that tap into students' existing skills, the book is designed to help students build a meta-awareness of language through critical digital literacy. Drawing on examples and activities from TikTok, Twitter, memes, texting, online videos, digital media, and more, the chapters feature lesson plans centered around real-world digital scenarios that will engage and inspire students.

Ideal for preservice and inservice English teachers, this book offers a blueprint for helping students use and evaluate language in the digital world and includes practical suggestions for using technology and rhetorical grammar to engage with and compose digital texts.

Darren Crovitz is Professor of English Education at Kennesaw State University, USA.

Michelle D. Devereaux is Associate Professor of English Education at Kennesaw State University, USA.

Clarice M. Moran is Assistant Professor of English Education at Appalachian State University, USA.

NEXT LEVEL GRAMMAR FOR A DIGITAL AGE

Teaching with Social Media and Online Tools for Rhetorical Understanding and Critical Creation

Darren Crovitz,
Michelle D. Devereaux,
and Clarice M. Moran

Co-published by Routledge and The National Council of Teachers of English

Cover image: © Getty Images

First published 2022
by Routledge
605 Third Avenue, New York, NY 10158

and by Routledge
4 Park Square, Milton Park, Abingdon, Oxon, OX14 4RN

Routledge is an imprint of the Taylor & Francis Group, an informa business

© 2022 Darren Crovitz, Michelle D. Devereaux, and Clarice M. Moran

The right of Darren Crovitz, Michelle D. Devereaux, and Clarice M. Moran to be identified as authors of this work has been asserted in accordance with sections 77 and 78 of the Copyright, Designs and Patents Act 1988.

All rights reserved. No part of this book may be reprinted or reproduced or utilised in any form or by any electronic, mechanical, or other means, now known or hereafter invented, including photocopying and recording, or in any information storage or retrieval system, without permission in writing from the publishers.

Trademark notice: Product or corporate names may be trademarks or registered trademarks, and are used only for identification and explanation without intent to infringe.

Library of Congress Cataloging-in-Publication Data
A catalog record for this title has been requested

ISBN: 978-0-367-72414-6 (hbk)
ISBN: 978-0-367-69755-6 (pbk)
ISBN: 978-1-003-15470-9 (ebk)

DOI: 10.4324/9781003154709

Typeset in Sabon
by KnowledgeWorks Global Ltd.

CONTENTS

Acknowledgments — vii

Introduction — 1

CHAPTER 1: **Positioning Digital Literacy in a Modern Context** — 3

CHAPTER 2: **Digital Literacy and Our Linguistic Worlds** — 13

SECTION I
Rhetorical Grammar in Digital Spaces — 21

CHAPTER 3: **1s and 0s: The Digital Nuts and Bolts** — 23

SECTION II
Language Moves in Digital Spaces — 63

CHAPTER 4: **Play or Be Played** — 65

CHAPTER 5: **Grammar at Work in Digital Texts** — 71

SECTION III
Counter the Narrative — 89

CHAPTER 6: **Using Digital Language to Change the World** — 91

CHAPTER 7: **Linguistic and Cultural Appropriation in Digital Contexts** — 109

Index — 117

ACKNOWLEDGMENTS

We're grateful to all those who've helped, directly and indirectly, with the vision for this book.

Thank you to all our English Education colleagues at Kennesaw State University and Appalachian State University, whose support and professionalism set the standard. We would like to specifically thank our colleague, Dr. Chris Palmer, for his feedback on portions of this book.

We are honored to work with excellent preservice and inservice teachers who keep us honest as we strive to learn more and do better. If the ideas, activities, and projects work in this book, it's because our students are always willing to question, experiment, and think through the possibilities and challenges toward guiding their own students, current and future, in a digital world. Thank you.

Once again, our editor at Routledge, Karen Adler, has been essential to this project. As our focus evolved through various drafts, she was always available for consultation and advice. We appreciate KGL's assistance in raising the quality of the manuscript. And thanks again to Kurt Austin and NCTE for their partnership.

Introduction

CHAPTER 1

Positioning Digital Literacy in a Modern Context

We thought for a long time how to position this opening chapter. As all writers do, we had to grapple with a pretty important question: *who is our audience*?

If you're picking up a book about digital grammar, we might assume that you're curious about technology—how it's impacting teaching and learning, or shifting our relationships with one another, or changing our sense of the world. Maybe you're an early adopter of all things digital, comfortable with communicating through digital tools and online spaces.[1] If that's the case, our hope is that this book will help you use that tech familiarity to pursue new language possibilities with your students.

If you're not a digital expert, however, we understand. Michelle is a relative rookie to online affordances with an attitude that might best be described as "ambivalent." Twenty years ago, when she was in her early 20s, she raged against the emerging technology that would become social media. *It will be the death of us! Our connections will break! We'll fall into our screens and forget our humanity! Oh, the horror!* Maybe you've had similar (if less dramatic) feelings.

Michelle isn't in that space anymore, but it took a while to get where she is now. Even with digital technology integrated into much of modern life, adjusting to the newness it brings—the shifts in gadgetry, spaces, interactions, communication, and culture—can be a challenge. If you're skeptical about (or uncomfortable with) technology and how it's taken up in the English language arts classroom, we hope this book provides a practical entryway as well as a critical perspective.

Wherever you are in your thinking about these subjects, there's no denying that digital technology is having a profound impact on how we live our lives, see the world, and understand one another. It's probably not something we can feasibly ignore as teachers, especially if we see our role as preparing creative and critically minded people for the future.

In this chapter, we'll explore some of the tensions between technology, language, and learning. Since that's a rather enormous intersection of topics, we'll try to focus on the essentials to keep the fear factor low. Our lens will center around what reading and writing look like in digital spaces and share some insight from the field of linguistics. Throughout, we'll weave in some history—of language, technology, and how folks react

---

1. Or maybe you had to buy this book for a class, and you just don't have a choice. It happens.

to the combination of the two. Even if you're a little suspicious about the influence of technology on literacy, you may be pleasantly surprised about what we share.

As a way to begin, it might be helpful to reflect on a few questions about what you believe:

- How do you view digital technology and those who embrace it, particularly adolescents?
- What role should digital tools, spaces, and communication play in school, if any?
- As our lives increasingly include digital dimensions, how do we best help young people grapple with the complexities and challenges that this reality brings?

KIDS THESE DAYS

Many of our own students—who are studying to be English teachers—are only a few years out of high school, about the same age as Michelle during her rage-against-the-digital-machine phase. Even so, some of them have pretty traditional assumptions about young people and technology, what might be called a "kids these days" attitude: kids these days have it easy, have little respect, are apathetic, spend too much time on their phones, have no goals. You know the complaint.

Almost every semester, Michelle shares this quotation on the board:

> Children now love luxury; they have bad manners, contempt for authority; they show disrespect for elders and love chatter in place of exercise. Children are now tyrants ... They contradict their parents, chatter before company ... and tyrannize their teachers.

Michelle's students resoundingly agree with this statement. *Kids these days*. She asks her students *when* they think this statement was made. A lot of them guess the 1950s or 1960s or earlier. Some guess within the last few years. Few get it right. This utterance is from Socrates, the Greek philosopher, about 2500 years ago. Michelle shows them this statement (and shares it here) to make a point: older people have been complaining about young people since forever.

It's easy to focus on the differences between today's generation and the world when we were growing up. Just for a moment, think about that time—your growing-up time. What was your daily routine like, and what were some of the new *technologies* on the scene when you were young? The WalkMan, perhaps? How about a multi-disc CD player? TVs and landlines so cheap you might have several in your house? Maybe even one (*gasp!*) in your bedroom? Now think about the adults in your life at that time. What were those grown-ups saying about your generation? What were the *kids these days* laments when you were the kid in that scenario?

Kids these days is not a new idea. Yes, of course adults looked at the adolescent-you and thought *what is wrong with the world*?!

We say all of this as a first step to embracing digital grammar. You have to get over the *kids these days* stereotype. Young folks today are no better or worse than any other generation—though they do face challenges far different from what we may have experienced. If we're going to teach effectively, we should seek to understand those challenges as well as the opportunities. And today, that means wrestling with the realities of a digital world.

BUT THINK ABOUT THE LANGUAGE! CAN'T WE SAVE THE LANGUAGE?!

The next argument we hear against digital anything might be called *But the language!* You know how this one goes: digital technology, and everything that's come with it, has caused an inevitable decline in literacy standards and the ability of young people to express themselves.

We'll be talking about digital reading and writing throughout this book, but let's focus here on the idea of "moral panic," a term that emerged frequently as we did background reading for this book (Scott, 2017; Shortis, 2007; Squires, 2010; Walsh, 2020). This term was coined by Stanley Cohen in the early 1970s and centered on "delinquency, youth cultures and subcultures, as well as football [i.e., soccer] hooliganism" (Luce, 2013, p. 395). Moral panics "tend to show underlying fears about issues that hit at the core of society" (Luce, p. 393), and you can probably name a few yourself. Rock 'n' roll, comic books, Dungeons & Dragons, gangsta rap, video games—all have triggered fearful reactions at some point, with detractors certain that these phenomena were signs of civilizational decay.

And now here comes the internet and digital language, which presents the "triple whammy of social panic, wherein adult fears about young people, language, and technology coincide" (Squires, 2010, p. 464). This reaction is, maybe, understandable. From a traditional schooling perspective, texting and emojis and meme language and other emerging forms can seem like a huge impediment to conventional literacy and even a threat to the pristine coherence of English. For some of us, it might seem like the language itself is under attack from the degrading influences of technology and the forces it has unleashed. But this conventional outlook rests on some pretty unstable ground. Thurlow (2018) reminds us that "English cannot really be lost because it was technically never found … There was never a neatly demarcated, unequivocally prescribed 'Golden Age of English' with a fully secured, unchanging standard" (p. 8). In short, English (like any language) has always been in flux.

And this particular moral panic—the idea that new ways of communicating alter the linguistic landscape for the worse—is not new. Since we gave Socrates a nod earlier, let's go back to the ancients for another relevant remark. This quotation comes from one of Socrates' followers, Plato:

> If men learn this, it will implant forgetfulness in their souls; they will cease to exercise memory because they rely on that which is written, calling things to remembrance no longer from within themselves, but by means of external marks. What you have discovered is a recipe not for memory, but for reminder. And it is no true wisdom that you offer your disciples, but only its semblance, for by telling them of many things without teaching them you will make them seem to know much, while for the most part they know nothing, and as men filled, not with wisdom, but with the conceit of wisdom, they will be a burden to their fellows.

You know what Plato's afraid of in this statement? *Writing.*

That's right. The written word. Plato believed that writing would keep people from remembering and thinking critically.

Just as we may need to reconsider the positioning of *kids these days*, we might also want to reconsider our attitudes toward language in the digital landscape. The fear of internet language seeping into standard language spaces began in the late 1990s and continues today (Squires, 2010). And often, public discourse around digital language is negative even with proof to the contrary (Thurlow, 2018). Michelle's dad likes to say, "never let the truth get in the way of a good story," and even though most of the tales about doom and gloom surrounding language are anecdotal (Herring, 2012), we all know that fear and suspense sells. Check out these headlines from the last decade or so:

"Texting Language Leaks into Schoolwork"[2]

- We particularly like this article because it begins with a glossary of text-speak—just to help you remember that the youths' way of communicating needs to be translated to be understood.

"Grammar and Spelling Erode in the Age of Texting—U Care?"[3]

- Some of our favorite terms in this article: "bad grammar habits" and "to forget the language rules they once lived by."

"Is Texting Making Us Bad Spellers?"[4]

- This article is a bait-and-switch (or "clickbait" if you like). Our blood pressure rises a little with the idea that *yes, texting is making us bad spellers*, but as it turns out, the article cites research that proves the exact opposite.

As is true with all news, exaggeration and fear draw attention, leaving us to worry about the language and its evident ruin. Thurlow (2018) sums it up nicely when he says, "The story of a 'new language' or of 'language threat' sells much better than a story about the gradual, inevitable 'evolution' of English" (p. 9).

However, as we'll discuss in this chapter and throughout this book, news headlines that spread language-based moral panics are often based on faulty assumptions and ingrained attitudes. The research tells different stories. And research matters.

So until we get to the research that might make you feel better (keep reading), let's stop dreading what's already happening: the slow and natural progression of language. Instead of fear, let's celebrate a new academic concept, *digital language*, because it isn't every day that fresh academic disciplines emerge (Crystal, 2005). Even better, your students know a lot about this topic, and inviting digital language into your classroom is yet another way to build on student strengths and interests. Indeed, McCulloch (2019) reminds us that

> When future historians look back on this era, they'll find our changes as fascinating as we now find innovative words from Shakespeare or Latin or Norman

---

2. Spandorf (2013).
3. Flammia (2015).
4. Nicholson (2009).

French. So let's adopt the perspective of these future historians now, and explore the revolutionary period in linguistic history that we're living through from a place of excitement and curiosity.

(p. 15)

We think this shift in attitude is ideal. We're living through an exciting period of history. Crystal (2005) explains that our language resources have *increased* through the internet (not decreased) and that hasn't happened in English's history since the Middle Ages and was largely lost with the standardization of English in the 18th century. Such innovation and creativity should be celebrated and explored. Hopefully, this book will give you some ways to do just that.

READING AND WRITING IN DIGITAL WORLDS: A BROAD OVERVIEW

Several years ago, Michelle spent an academic year in the Czech Republic. When she arrived, she was still a bit of a purist in her texting. She never used emoticons or emojis because she thought words were powerful enough to get the job done. (Oh, how our pride can get in the way of our own progress!) She quickly realized, however, that her texts could easily be misconstrued by others: her new colleagues, her children's teachers, and her newfound friends, all of whom spoke English as their second (or third or fourth) language. It was a real-life concern that needed a real-life solution. To clarify her meaning, Michelle began using emoticons and emojis in her texts.

We tell this story to introduce a pretty important point: reading and writing in digital worlds isn't dichotomous. Words alone weren't working for Michelle—effective communication didn't always happen. So she had to embrace other communicative modes. In digital spaces, reading, writing, and speaking rarely exist as separate modes; rather, they merge in new ways to enable effective communication.[5] This melding doesn't happen haphazardly; instead, it's a purposeful feature of the *multimodal* nature of digital communication.

Below, we discuss a few language moves in digital spaces, contextualizing them in linguistics and history. This discussion is not meant to be exhaustive or completely inclusive.[6] Our goal is to show that language changes, in all spaces, constantly: it has done so forever and will continue to do so forever. We should also clarify that while we've tried to group some concepts together in easily consumable bites, there are no clearly defined boundaries in digital language. Spelling affects mechanics affects grammar affects typography and then back again. Each aspect of language affects other aspects in creative and playful ways. Of course, playful language—creative language—isn't just found in digital spaces. When Michelle teaches her grammar classes and discusses "rules" of language, she always notes that nothing in language, even the codified "standard" of traditional schooling, is true 100% of the time.[7] Why? Because no matter the context in which

---

5. As we will discuss below, this merging of reading, writing, and speaking isn't new at all. It was happening way before "digital" was a thing.
6. For a thorough exploration of modern digital language and some cool contextualization with linguistics and history, check out *Because Internet: Understanding the New Rules of Language* by Gretchen McCulloch.
7. No matter what worksheets may lead you to believe.

we use language—school, digital, social, etc.—language lives. It changes and flexes and pretty much just refuses to be pinned down. And we think that is pretty fabulous.

Sounds, Words, and Spellings (and Typography for Good Measure)

The fancy linguistic term for spelling is orthography, and spelling in digital spaces has been a long-term concern of language purists. There was a fear that the changes in spelling online and in text messages would ruin students' ability to write (see the news articles mentioned earlier). Luckily, a lot of studies debunk that myth. Research has shown that phonetic (sound) abbreviations like *2nite* actually demonstrate a positive connection between phonetic knowledge and reading (Adams, 1990; Snowling, 2000). In fact, unintentional nonstandard misspellings are pretty uncommon among first-language English speakers (Herring, 2012). Research has shown little evidence that texting affects an adolescent's spelling ability, and, indeed, there are strong relationships between texting and other measures of their English ability, such as reading (Plester et al., 2009). Recent research has found that increased time online helps students (1) code-switch between the language of the internet and the language of the university classroom, and (2) increase their self-confidence in their writing ability (Parrella et al., 2021).

So now that we've (hopefully) persuaded you that the language of the internet and texting isn't destroying the English language, let's look at what happens with sounds, words, and spellings in digital spaces. Even in this new domain, some standardization is apparent.[8]

Playfulness and creativity drive these "non-standard" spellings. They aren't the random nonsense of lazy language users—these words, created through "play," follow some old rules for word creation, such as initialism, acronyms, clipping, and blending (Curzan & Adams, 2012). We also can't relegate playful uses of language to informal spaces either—as history continues to show us.

A letter that begins "Lord Fisher to the Right Hon. Winston Churchill; My Dear Winston" might seem like a pretty formal space (see Figure 1.1). However, it is in this letter to Churchill that we see the first use of "O.M.G." in print, way back in 1917.

Table 1.1 Non-Standard Spelling's Standardization (Based on Shortis, 2007)

Space-Saving Moves	Spell It Like You Speak It	Orthography as Art
Omission of vowels (*gd* for *good*)	Eye dialect (*tuff* for *tough*)	Emoticons
Letter and number homophones (*r* for *are*; *2* for *too, two,* or *to*)	Accent simulation or blending (*gonna* for *going to*)	:) (smiley face)
Initialism and acronyms for key bindings and phrases (*g2g* for *got to go*)	Semiotic features such as all caps to indicate volume	Art @}->-- (rose)
Clipping of words (*congrats* for *congratulations*; *info* for *information*)	Reduplication for emphasis (*hhhhheeeeeeelllllllooooooo*)	Use of color, movement, pictorial imagery
Sensible respellings (*thru* for *through*; *nite* for *night*)		

---

8. Although, as we warned earlier, all rules of language are slippery and can change depending on context—see Table 1.1 more as a guide than the Truth.

LORD FISHER TO THE RIGHT HON. WINSTON CHURCHILL.

MY DEAR WINSTON,
I AM here for a few days longer before rejoining my "Wise men" at Victory House—

"The World forgetting,
By the World forgot!"

but some Headlines in the newspapers have utterly upset me! Terrible!!
"The German Fleet to assist the Land operations in the Baltic."
"Landing the German Army South of Reval."
We are five times stronger at Sea than our enemies and here is a small Fleet that we could gobble up in a few minutes playing the great vital Sea part of landing an Army in the enemies' rear and probably capturing the Russian Capital by Sea!
This is "Holding the ring" with a vengeance!
Are we really incapable of a big Enterprise?
I hear that a new order of Knighthood is on the tapis —O.M.G. (Oh! My God!)—Shower it on the Admiralty!!

Yours,
FISHER.
9/9/17.

Figure 1.1 Letter to Winston Churchill

In 1913, we see similar orthographic play in the magazine of the Eton College East End[9] boys project (as cited in Shortis, 2007, p. 24):

ROT, YET NOT.

D R friends, I humbly beg of U
    2 tarry and 2 read,
And I promise I'll apologise
    2 U-that's if there's need.
My native home's in 0 I 0 –
    "Some place" I guess you'll say;
But, gentlemen, I tell U this:
    0 I 0's in U.S.A.

In fact, we can go back even further than 1913 to see examples of writing efficiency. Medieval scribes invented new symbols such as & and %. The Romans inscribed coins

---

9. That's right—*the Eton College* in England, founded in 1440 by King Henry VI. A pretty formal space, we would imagine.

and statues with SPQR instead of the full *Senatus Populusque Romanus*. And during the Renaissance, obsessed with Latin, users of English adopted Latin abbreviations like e.g. (for example) and ibid. (in the same reference already cited) (McCulloch, 2019, p. 10). As McCulloch reminds us, "'standard' language and 'correct' spellings are collective agreements, not eternal truths, and collective agreements can change" (p. 46). Or, as our little walk down linguistic history lane has shown us, maybe not change that much after all.

Syntax (Grammar)

In this section, we'll give you a quick overview of how digital language interacts with syntax and mechanics and how the lines between speech and writing blur in these spaces. We think it's important to begin with a little more research, in part because we know the concern of student writing is still in the forefront as we walk through this chapter. However, take heart. The research around grammar and digital language is just as positive as that around spelling and digital language.

In 2014, a group of researchers (Wood et al., 2014) published a study in which they administered grammar tests to adolescents and adults twice over the course of a year. The researchers wanted to gauge if and how the participants' use of textisms *affected their performance on the grammar tests*. (That last part is italicized because it's important.) While textisms (like "wanna") popped up every once in a while, they didn't affect overall scores. In fact, researchers found no association between grammar violations and literacy skills. That seems important.

We sometimes see textisms in our students' writing at the college level; no doubt the same is true for English teachers at the middle and high school levels. The research suggests that such usage is best treated as a matter of context and appropriate fit rather than as a broader threat to a student's development as a writer. Textisms (like other language choices) work in specific situations but not in others, and their use can be appropriate in many digital situations. We can help students assess context so that they make informed choices whenever they compose anything, from a social media post to a formal essay.

So now that we know that digital language isn't ruining English, let's talk about what's actually happening on a sentence level with this new way of using language in the modern world.

In 2016, a group of researchers published something we find interesting: omission of words (or in linguistic speak, the use of elliptical sentences). Let's pause here and do some definitions and explanations. We all know the ellipses because we teach them when we're teaching direct quotations (…). Those three periods indicate that in our quotation, we've purposefully left out some words from the original text, but what we've cited is still understandable. We do something similar in our speech frequently as in this exchange:

Number 1: When are you going to the movies?
Number 2: After dinner.

If you were person Number 1 in this scenario, you wouldn't think twice about Number 2's answer. "After dinner" is a completely sensible reply to the question because it's an elliptical sentence. It's understood in the context of Number 1's question to actually mean "I am going to the movies after dinner." Language users are good at figuring out ways to communicate concisely. Why use complete sentences in such situations if you don't have to?

Since the lines between writing and speech are often blurred in digital spaces, elliptical communication is common, and a group of researchers (van Dijk et al., 2016) wanted to know if such ellipticity affected adolescents' grammar performance. Turns out, the more words children omitted in their text messages, the *better* their performance on the grammar task.

How is it that students can make supposed standardized English "errors" in their writing and still have a larger understanding of language? Because encouraging play and creativity in digital spaces allows for an overall better understanding of English. If you're all about communicating as effectively as possible (meaning, knowing what words you can omit while still ensuring that the message makes sense), that's some useful meta-knowledge about language.

Mechanics (Punctuation)

Historically, there have been two schools of punctuation: the typographical and the syntactic. Typographical punctuation began with medieval scribes,[10] who needed ways to mark pauses or stops for priests who read their writings aloud. Meanwhile, syntactic punctuation, which conquered the mainstream world in the 18th century with the push toward standardizing language, is concerned with rule-based grammatical construction (Brown, 2020). However, experts today agree that punctuation is ultimately about understanding. As Brown notes, Henry James would be completely unintelligible without his commas, and Ernest Hemingway needs little more than a period (n.p.). Pause marking in writing has long been intuitive. From Jane Austen's commas to Emily Dickinson's dashes, humans like to make writing sound human (McCulloch, 2019).

The line between punctuation and speaking has been hazy since the beginning. While we don't use punctuation explicitly when we speak, we all grew up hearing sentences like "She is trouble with a capital T" and "I said you can't go. Period." McCulloch (2019) found two examples of spoken punctuation from the 1890s: "He would not flinch one comma of the law" and "There was a very big question mark in [her] voice" (p. 130).

And while the spoken hashtag is fairly recent (as a digital tool, hashtags first appeared on Twitter in 2007), the hashtag itself originated in Rome where folks abbreviated "libra pondo" or "pound in weight" as "lb" (Panko, 2017). Hashtags on Twitter have moved beyond their initial function as a search tool for grouped posts to a spoken pragmatic purpose. Research suggests that spoken hashtags serve to clarify feelings and offer meta-commentary on a situation, while their textual use online provides context for messages (Scott, 2017). Pretty interesting.

---

10. For an interesting history of the comma, see Chapter 3.

CONCLUSION

Ultimately, humans want to communicate successfully, a need that can blur the lines of traditionally demarcated linguistic spaces. However, these borders aren't real anyway because a set of usage rules isn't how real humans use language in real spaces. Are rules codified in grammar and style books? Yes. But when two friends are sharing a cup of coffee, or when a mother and her child are speaking, *whatever is effective* becomes the rule.

Ideally, this chapter has provided just enough history and linguistics to support the idea of evolution, creativity, flexibility, and playfulness as central to language use. As we'll see, grammar in digital spaces involves all of these concepts and more.

REFERENCES

Adams, M. J. (1990). *Beginning to read: Thinking and learning about print*. Bradford.
Breakstone, J., McGrew, S., Smith, M., Ortega, T., & Wineburg, S. (2018). Why we need a new approach to teaching digital literacy. *Phi Delta Kappan, 99*(18), 27–32. https://doi.org/10.1177/0031721718762419
Brown, T. J. (2020, January 3). Punctuation. *Encyclopedia Britannica*. https://www.britannica.com/topic/punctuation
Buckingham, D. (2016). Defining digital literacy: What do young people need to know about digital media? *Nordic Journal of Digital Literacy, 3*(12), n.p. https://www.idunn.no/dk/2015/Jubileumsnummer/defining_digital_literacy_-_what_do_young_people_need_to_kn
Crystal, D. (2005). The scope of internet linguistics. Paper presented virtually at the *American Association for the Advancement of Science*.
Curzan, A., & Adams, M. (2012). *How English works: A linguistic introduction*. Pearson.
Flammia, D. (2015, April 1). Grammar and spelling erode in the age of texting—U care? *New Jersey, 101.5*. https://nj1015.com/where-has-all-the-grammar-gone/
Hauer, T. (2017). Technological determinism and new media. *International Journal of English, Literature and Social Sciences, 2*(2), 1–4.
Herring, S. C. (2012). Grammar and electronic communication. *The encyclopedia of applied linguistics* (n.p.). Wiley. https://doi.org/10.1002/9781405198431.wbeal0466
Houston, K. (2015, September 2). The mysterious origins of punctuation. *BBC*. https://www.bbc.com/culture/article/20150902-the-mysterious-origins-of-punctuation
Luce, A. (2013). Moral panics: Reconsidering journalism's responsibilities. In K. Fowler-Watt & S. Allan (Eds.), *Journalism: New challenges* (pp. 393–409). Centre for Journalism and Communication Research, Bournemouth University.
McCulloch, G. (2019). *Because internet: Understanding the new rules of language*. Penguin Random House.
Nicholson, C. (2009, September 23). Is texting making us bad spellers? *Scientific American*. https://www.scientificamerican.com/podcast/episode/is-texting-making-us-bad-spellers-09-09-23/
Pangrazio, L. (2016). Reconceptualizing critical digital literacy. *Discourse: Studies in the Cultural Politics of Education, 37*(2), 163–174. https://doi.org/10.1080/01596306.2014.942836
Panko, B. (2017, August 23, 2017). A decade ago, the hashtag reshaped the internet. *Smithsonian Magazine*. https://www.smithsonianmag.com/smart-news/decade-ago-hashtag-reshaped-internet-180964605/
Parrella, J., Leggette, H. R., & Redwine, T. (2021). Measuring the correlation between digital media usage and students' perceived writing ability: Are they related? *Research in Learning Technology, 29*, 1–14. https://doi.org/10.25304/rlt.v29.2506
Plester, B., Wood, C., & Joshi, P. (2009). Exploring the relationship between children's knowledge of text message abbreviations and school literacy outcomes. *British Journal of Developmental Psychology, 27*, 145–161.
Scott, K. (2017). "Hashtags work everywhere": The pragmatic functions of spoken hashtags. *Discourse, Context, & Media, 22*, 57–64. https://doi.org/10.1016/j.dcm.2017.07.002
Shortis, T. (2007). Gr8 txtpectations: The creativity of text spelling. *English Drama Media*, 21–26.
Snowling, M. (2000). *Dyslexia: 2nd edition*. Blackwell.
Spandorf, E. (2013, November 13). Texting language leaks into school work. *Northwest Arkansas Democrat Gazette*. https://www.nwaonline.com/news/2013/nov/04/texting-language-leaks-school-work/
Squires, L. (2010). Enregistering internet language. *Language in Society, 39*(4), 457–492. https://doi.org/10.1017/S0047404510000412
Thurlow, C. (2018). Digital discourse: Locating language in new/social media. In J. Burgess, T. Poell & A. Marwick (Eds.), *Handbook of social media* (pp. 135–145). Sage.
van Dijk, C. N., van Witteloostuijn, M., Vasić, N., & Avrutin, S. (2016). The influence of texting language on grammar and executive functions in primary school children. *PLoS ONE, 11*(3). https://doi.org/10.1371/journal.pone.0152409
Walsh, J. P. (2020). Social media and moral panics: Assessing the effects of technological change on societal reaction. *International Journal of Cultural Studies, 23*(6), 840–859. https://doi.org/10.1177/1367877920912257
Wood, C., Kemp, N., & Waldron, S. (2014). Exploring the longitudinal relationships between the use of grammar in text messaging and performance on grammatical tasks. *British Journal of Developmental Psychology, 32*, 415–429. https://doi.org/10.1111/bjdp.12049

CHAPTER 2

Digital Literacy and Our Linguistic Worlds

Without people, language isn't a thing. From this fact, it's not a huge leap to understand that language is shaped by those who use it, in the contexts in which it's used. Because language involves people, it's also intimately connected to identity and power. That's what this chapter is all about: the social contexts of digital language.

THE SOCIOLINGUISTICS OF DIGITAL LITERACY

Scholars have written for decades about how language is connected to power structures, communities, cultures, and identities (Baker-Bell, 2020; Edwards, 1985; Fairclough, 1989, 1992; Gee, 2008; Heath, 1983; Lee, 2007; Smitherman, 1977 [really, this is a short list—there's *a lot* of research in this area]). So as soon as communication took to the internet, manifestations of power, society, and identity came along too: what we believe, what other folks want us to believe, who we hope to be, who we want to be with, and so on. The discussion below isn't an exhaustive journey into the sociolinguistic landscape of the digital, more like an introductory framework important for both framing the rest of this book and teaching about language in digital spaces.

While we divide the discussion below into power, society, and identity, please understand that these terms cannot truly be separated, nor do they completely cover the landscape of sociolinguistic digital literacy. These concepts overlap, and there are other sociological aspects that complicate and complement these terms, such as history, culture, and institutions. People and language are a messy, complex topic. We've organized them here as we've done in previous works for simplicity and consistency (Crovitz & Devereaux, 2017, 2019; Devereaux, 2015). Orienting discussions around power, society, and identity can be a helpful gloss for understanding applied sociolinguistic ideas.

The Power of Language and the Language of Power

Power in digital environments takes various forms. We could focus on power and access to online spaces—who has it and how it's defined across well-known lines of inequity in the United States, e.g., socio-economic status, mother's education level, race, etc. (Breakstone et al., 2019; Common Sense Media, 2020[1]). We could also

---

1. https://www.commonsensemedia.org/about-us/news/press-releases/as-online-videos-dominate-young-kids-screen-time-youtube-exposes-them

consider representation—who has the power to make their voices heard and whose voices are marginalized (Buckingham, 2016). Such considerations highlight the importance of understanding and managing the relationship between language and power (Pangrazio, 2016). In our example below, we briefly discuss a way by which institutions use the relationship between digital language and power to influence people's beliefs and actions.

Power in Silos of Information

Social media is designed to group people with others who are like-minded and then put individualized information and stories in front of them (Walsh, 2020). This can be super problematic because it means people can end up reading stories and viewing images that only reflect their personal ideologies.[2] This is where the ideas of "silos of information" or "echo chambers" emerge. When the information on the internet is channeled and curated to fit our own personal concerns and ideologies, then certain existing power structures are maintained. We aren't asked to consider other people's opinions because we don't have to.

Democracy depends on accessing reliable information (Breakstone et al., 2019). We need access to agreed-upon facts if we are to make informed decisions. If, instead, we only seek out information that confirms our prior beliefs regardless of fact, then reliable information gives way to propaganda. That's why, throughout this book, we'll discuss the importance of teaching students to read critically on the internet. Doing so ensures that students understand that while verifiable scientific facts certainly exist, the idea of *one objective truth* doesn't exist, that all information is couched in ideologies (Buckingham, 2016). Moving to this critical point allows us to question how existing in *silos of information* supports traditional power structures and hinders our ability to critically question those power structures.

The Social Life of Digital Language

We engage with language in digital spaces as a cultural form (Buckingham, 2016), and how we engage with this language marks us as part of a group. Squires (2010) discusses how different language uses on the internet go through a process called *enregisterment*, which means that language variation and structure are used to define in-group or out-group varieties.

This means that when discussing digital language with students, we need to understand that their use of digital language is purposeful, denoting in-group status (*Hey, look! My language looks like yours—that means I belong*). On the internet, there exist innumerable communities of practice—groups who use specific language (or images and symbols) in specific ways to mark their belonging. For example, members of some politically right-leaning groups use the term, "blackpill" to describe a fatalistic attitude about the direction of society.[3] In fact, during the 2020 U.S. election, the alt-right developed its

---

2. For a deeper dive into this idea, including activities to promote discussion in the classroom, see Chapter 5.
3. In opposition to "red pill," which grants access to the hidden truth (from *The Matrix*).

own set of symbols and language to signal belonging.[4] But this type of in-group marking has been happening for a long time. Two thousand years ago, early Christians adopted the sign of the fish to alert others to their affiliation. But when we bring digital language into the classroom as a point of study, we can encourage students to examine their own language use and how it marks their affiliation with a group. Such explorations also allow for questions of access: Who has access to these groups? Is this access equitable?

Cultural Appropriation in Digital Spaces

The internet allows information to travel quickly, and that includes new language uses. Often, new slang gains mainstream popularity without consideration for its origins or credit to its originators. As many have noted (Baker-Bell, 2020; Hill, 2008), slang words and phrases often have their roots in Black language. For example, "tea" (meaning gossip) originated decades ago in the Black gay community, and the phrase "and I oop" is derived from a 2015 video with Black drag queen Jasmine Masters (Tenbarge, 2020).[5] In Chapter 7, we dig into linguistic and cultural appropriation, offering frameworks to invite discussion in the classroom.

Performing Identity in Digital Spaces

How we choose to use language in digital spaces represents our choices, habits, and sense of identity (Shortis, 2007). As we learn new ways to communicate, we can adopt new social identities (Janks, 2000) and can concern ourselves with *authenticity*, which is an interactional phenomenon in digital spaces. To be authentic is to pass as part of the group (as in the in-group status mentioned earlier), and "passing" is dependent upon the context (Hower, 2018).

This is a lot to maneuver: considerations of authenticity and in-group status, considerations of our choices and habits, and how we present ourselves to the world. With innumerable choices of identities and groups to align with, discussions of digital language seem like a critical concept for the classroom. If our students are contending with not only their own representation, but group membership, as well as deciding what truth is (see the *power* discussion above), then offering students tools to thoughtfully move through these spaces seems like an important part of the English classroom.

Identity in Digital Spaces

People aren't the only ones concerned about online identity. Corporations are too. They understand that identity and authenticity sell. Norman Fairclough (1989) put a name to this quite a long time ago: *synthetic personalization*—how corporations present themselves in online spaces as actual people. Companies acting as individuals with specific

---

4. We're going to share an article here that discusses the specifics of this language, but we also have to note that the fear-mongering in the title of this article is similar to what we discussed in Chapter 1. *Oh no! A group you don't understand has a language you don't understand and here's a guide to show how scary it is.* https://qz.com/1092037/the-alt-right-is-creating-its-own-dialect-heres-a-complete-guide/

5. https://www.insider.com/internet-slang-origin-i-oop-meaning-sksk-vsco-girls-stans-2020-1

identities can be problematic for consumers, particularly adolescents, however profitable this tactic might be. One easy example is the phenomenon of certain companies "roasting" one another on Twitter. When Wendy's, the fast-food burger joint, playfully insults another fast-food operation, it's not the company performing snark but rather a human employee, nameless and faceless. This type of Janus-faced marketing is an important point of discussion in the classroom. What does it mean for corporations to use identity-markers in online spaces, and how does it complicate ideas about authenticity and credibility?

Throughout this book, we will give you tools to have these discussions. We will provide in-depth frameworks and lesson ideas. We believe that understanding ourselves and the worlds in which we and others live is a necessary facet of modern life. And when we say "world," we are, of course, considering the digital worlds that we are all part of.

CRITICAL DIGITAL LITERACY

In 2019, Common Sense Media released a report that found that children 8–12 years old spend an average of almost five hours a day in front of a screen (4 hours and 44 minutes) and that children 13–18 years old spend over seven hours a day in front of a screen (7 hours and 22 minutes). This time doesn't account for using screens for homework and schoolwork (as cited in Pappas, 2020).

This kind of statistic can easily lead to bemoaning the state of the world and falling into a *kids these days* narrative (see Chapter 1). We hope we've convinced you that when you were a kid, the adults in your world worried just as much about MTV or something similar.[6] We don't share these statistics about screen time to strike fear in your hearts but rather to say, "this is the world today; now how are we going to help students be successful?"

While your students could teach you amazing things about the online spaces they navigate on a daily basis, as teachers, we have to remember that consumption doesn't necessarily equate with critical thinking. Students may spend a lot of time online and have many valuable things to teach about their digital worlds, but that doesn't mean that they understand how power and identity is intricately bound in online spaces. However, that's where the classroom, and where this book, comes in.

WHAT IS CRITICAL DIGITAL LITERACY?

The idea of *critical literacy* has been around for a while (see Janks, 2000) and is based on the sociocultural theory of education, which is essentially what we've been talking about in this chapter: language can't be separated from the people and contexts *in which* and *through which* it is used. Furthermore, these uses are bound in questions of power, culture, society, history, identity—you get the idea. So when we talk about *critical digital literacy*, it isn't a big move. We're focusing on how language manifests in these critical ways in digital spaces.

---

6. Maybe your great-great grandparents fretted, for instance, about women showing their ankles in public. There's a historical club on Jekyll Island on the coast of Georgia that has extravagant mansions from the early 1900s. One of these houses has a porch that was specially designed for a horse-drawn carriage to sit flush. This way, when women disembarked from the carriage, they could step directly on to the porch in order to avoid (*gasp!*) showing their ankles.

While we applaud teachers and schools who bring in digital activities and lessons into their classrooms, we also believe that education *about* digital spaces should be part of education *with* or *through* digital spaces (Buckingham, 2016). In other words, it isn't just about using Twitter, but about including critical conversations about what Twitter is, how it's used, and to what ends. Explorations of the *who* and *why* behind digital creation, questions of invisible commercial influences, inquiries into our own roles as audiences in digital spaces, and examinations into what it means to be a digital consumer: these types of forays are the beginnings of teaching critical digital literacy in your classroom.

Integrating digital consumerism is a key component of critical digital literacy. For example, why don't we question the accepted language around digital media? How do words like "*free, friend, link, like, community, share, collaboration,* and *open* actually represent the digital context" (Pazgrazio, 2016, p. 172)? Such terms indicate a human connection in a digital space. How does this situate the social platform that uses these terms? How does it situate the users of these platforms? And how does this all give the feeling of genuine human connection?

We have to also embrace the fact that critical digital literacy does not, indeed cannot, equate to a checklist. Perhaps you know what we're talking about—those common checklists used to assess a website's veracity:

> *Is the website .edu or .org?*
> CHECK!
> *Is the information up to date with recent citations?*
> CHECK!
> *Does the website have an "About" page?*
> CHECK!

Congratulations! Then you've found a reliable source!

We hate to break it to you, but these types of checklists don't really work (Breakstone et al., 2018, 2019; Buckingham, 2016). Much like the grammar worksheets we've argued against in previous books (Crovitz & Devereaux, 2017, 2019), checklists look like school, so they feel safe. But, again, like those grammar worksheets, they don't really teach what you think they're teaching. In fact, we would argue that checklists are more detrimental than grammar worksheets: they can give students a false sense of security that the information they're reading online is true and has been tested for its truth, when really what they're reading may be propaganda.

This is important. Our students are spending a lot of time in front of a screen every day. It isn't our job to change this reality (or even bemoan the fact that this is the way things are). Our job is to make sure that those hours spent online come with a critical lens—a lens that allows our students to read beyond a checklist, to understand who is trying to sell them what, ideologically or otherwise.

The research paints a mixed picture of how our students currently read online. One study notes that "middle school students mistook advertisements for news stories. High schoolers were unable to verify social media accounts. College students blithely accepted a website's description of itself" (Breakstone et al., 2018). Other research, meanwhile, indicates that young people are far less likely to share online disinformation than senior citizens (Guess, Nadler, & Tucker, 2019). If democracy does depend on the ability to access reliable information, we should probably be spending more time helping our students to become critical readers online (and maybe offering lessons for grandma too).

The problems with checklists are that they are an analog solution to a digital problem (Breakstone et al., 2018), and they imply that diligent searching will reveal an objective truth (Buckingham, 2016). Breakstone et al. (2019) found that checklists encourage vertical reading, meaning they ask students to examine the website thoroughly, assuming that the answers to its veracity are embedded somewhere in the website itself. Unfortunately, it is very easy for special interest groups to buy a *.org* website and pay someone to make it look professional and believable. Breakstone et al. (2018) write:

> … over 96% [of the student participants] never learned about the ties between a climate change website and the fossil fuel industry. Instead of investigating the group behind the site, students were duped by weak signs of credibility: the website's 'look,' it's top-level domain, or the content on it's About page. Each of these features is ludicrously easy to game.
>
> (p. 21)

The researchers didn't just examine how students tested a website's veracity; they also examined how fact-checkers moved across the internet to test websites. Rather than moving down a page, like students did, fact-checkers moved laterally, meaning they opened multiple tabs searching for background information found on the website itself. For example, fact-checkers would open another tab and search for the name of the group associated with the website and dig in there. These types of moves show that fossil fuel industries can fund bogus "climate change" websites, and multi-billion-dollar corporations can fund sites devoted to minimum wage issues. Students' fluency with digital devices doesn't mean they are sophisticated judges of the information they read (Breakstone et al., 2018). That's what the classroom is for.

CONCLUSION

If you are still nurturing a *kids these days* mindset, some of what you read in these two chapters might dismay you, shock you, or just bum you out. But this is the state of the world. This is where we are. And this is where your students are as well. As with all things education, we encourage you to embrace and celebrate everything your students know of the digital world. Invite that expertise into your classroom, and then help them develop the lenses that will make them critical citizens of the world.

REFERENCES

Baker-Bell, A. (2020). *Linguistic justice: Black language, literacy, identity, and pedagogy*. Routledge. https://doi.org/10.4324/9781315147383

Breakstone, J., McGrew, S., Smith, M., Ortega, T., & Wineburg, S. (2018). Why we need a new approach to teaching digital literacy. *Phi Delta Kappan*, 99(18), 27–32. https://doi.org/10.1177/0031721718762419

Breakstone, J., Smith, M., Wineburg, S., Rapaport, A., Carle, J., Garland, M., & Saavedra, A. (2019). Students' civic online reasoning: A national portrait. Stanford History Education Group & Gibson Consulting. https://purl.stanford.edu/gf151tb4868

Buckingham, D. (2016). Defining digital literacy: What do young people need to know about digital media? *Nordic Journal of Digital Literacy*, *3*(12), n.p. https://www.idunn.no/dk/2015/Jubileumsnummer/defining_digital_literacy_-_what_do_young_people_need_to_kn

Common Sense Media (2020). *The Common sense census: Media use by tweens and teens*. https://www.commonsensemedia.org/sites/default/files/uploads/research/census_researchreport.pdf

Crovitz, D., & Devereaux, M. D. (2017). *Grammar to get things done: A practical guide for teachers anchored in real-world usage*. Routledge and NCTE. https://doi.org/10.4324/9781315544410

Crovitz, D., & Devereaux, M. D. (2019). *More grammar to get things done: Daily lessons for teaching grammar in context*. Routledge and NCTE. https://doi.org/10.4324/9780429202711

Devereaux, M. D. (2015). *Teaching about dialect variations and language in secondary English classrooms: Power, prestige, and prejudice*. Routledge. https://doi.org/10.4324/9780203581261

Edwards, J. (1985). *Language, society and identity*. Basil Blackwell Publishers.

Fairclough, N. (1989). *Language and power*. Longman.

Gee, J. P. (2008). *Social linguistics and literacies: Ideology in discourses* (3rd ed.). Routledge.

Guess, A., Nadler, K., & Tucker, J. (2019). Less than you think: Prevalence and predictors of fake news dissemination on Facebook. *Science Advances*, *5*(9). http://advances.sciencemag.org/content/5/1/eaau4586

Heath, S. B. (1983). *Ways with words: Language, life, and work in communities and classrooms*. Cambridge University Press.

Hill, J. H. (2008). Linguistic appropriation: The history of White racism is embedded in American English. *The everyday language of White racism*. Blackwell.

Hower, K. (2018). The construction of authenticity in corporate social media. Language@Internet, 15. https://www.languageatinternet.org/articles/2018/hower

Janks, H. (2000). Domination, access, diversity and design: A synthesis for critical literacy education. *Educational Review*, *52*(2), 175–186. https://doi.org/10.1080/713664035

Lee, C. D. (2007). *Culture, literacy, and learning: Taking bloom in the midst of the whirlwind*. Teachers College Press.

Pangrazio, L. (2016). Reconceptualizing critical digital literacy. *Discourse: Studies in the Cultural Politics of Education*, *37*(2), 163–174. https://doi.org/10.1080/01596306.2014.942836

Pappas, S. (2020, April 1). What do we really know about kids and screens? *American Psychological Association*. https://www.apa.org/monitor/2020/04/cover-kids-screens#:~:text=A%20report%20released%20in%20October,each%20day%20(The%20Common%20Sense

Shortis, T. (2007). Gr8 txtpectations: The creativity of text spelling. *English Drama Media*, 8, 21–26.

Smitherman, G. (1977). *Talkin and testifyin: The language of Black America*. Wayne State University Press.

Squires, L. (2010). Enregistering internet language. *Language in Society*, *39*(4), 457–492. https://doi.org/10.1017/S0047404510000412

Tenbarge, K. (2020, January 26). From 'periodt' to 'and I oop,' the most common stan culture and VSCO girl slang is rooted in cultural appropriation. *Insider*. https://www.insider.com/internet-slang-origin-i-oop-meaning-sksk-vsco-girls-stans-2020-1

Walsh, J. P. (2020). Social media and moral panics: Assessing the effects of technological change on societal reaction. *International Journal of Cultural Studies*, *23*(6), 840–859. https://doi.org/10.1177/1367877920912257

SECTION I

Rhetorical Grammar in Digital Spaces

CHAPTER 3

1s and 0s: The Digital Nuts and Bolts

When actress Emma Watson (who famously portrayed Hermione Granger in the *Harry Potter* films) commissioned a fake tattoo in 2018, she had hoped to pay homage to the Women's Movement with the sentiment "Time's Up." Alas, her tattoo ended up reading "Times Up" instead. "Fake tattoo proofreading position available," Watson subsequently tweeted, "Experience with apostrophes a must" (Watson, 2018). In 2016, *ABC News* tweeted about presidential candidate Hillary Clinton's future debate plan, noting that "Clinton invited several people to the debate, including Mark Cuban, a 9/11 survivor and a domestic abuse survivor" (ABC News, 2016). The lack of an Oxford comma in the tweet might have led some to wonder if Cuban had been through more than just a few seasons of *Shark Tank*. Similar comma trouble struck again in a Facebook post about a high school reunion, when one of the group members floated a recommendation concerning appropriate attire: "don't wear black people."

Of course, grammar gaffes abound online, where we publish quickly—and often without the benefit of a built-in proofreader. The standard reaction to such errors echoes an age-old tendency: not-so-subtle mockery and a wag of the finger at this language sloppiness (sometimes with a *tsk tsk* for good measure). But before we fall into our old mocking, wagging, and *tsk*ing ways, let's consider something important: mistakes like those described above rarely result in an incomprehensible message. We know (or we can figure out easily enough from the context) what a person was *attempting* to communicate. And since the whole point of language is the exchange of meaning, bemoaning surface miscues in online public spaces isn't really much more than a kind of digital public shaming.

In pre-internet times, most of the errors, misspellings, and creative punctuation in our semi-private messages had a pretty short lifespan—about as long as it took to toss that handwritten note in the wastebasket. Now our casual communication is subject to the eternity of the never-completely-erasable internet. Digital expression has the immediacy of speech but little of its ephemerality (even with disappearing messaging apps) and is probably even more permanent now than conventional writing. The modern internet blends both the personal and public through print, verbal, visual, and multimodal means. We can post (or livestream) an idea on a whim, only seconds after having the thought. While such immediacy can lead to grammar gaffes like those discussed above, it can also have bigger implications. Namely, it has transformed how we understand current events and crises, such as the riots in Hong Kong in 2019 and the murder of George Floyd in 2020, yielding a type of first-person news response to societal events that eclipses slower mainstream journalism.

One thing is for sure: digital technologies are providing fascinating new territory where existing and emergent literacies are flourishing. At the same time, however, new language-based threats have arisen as well, far more worrisome than any misplaced comma.

According to the Pew Research Center (2019), the vast majority of Americans now get at least some of their news and information from an online website or other platform, including Facebook and Twitter. It is not inconceivable to think that in the future, resources such as newspapers, magazines, and books printed on paper will be obsolete—relegated to the status of quaint antiques—while a hastily written tweet or Instagram post will be read into perpetuity as a fact. Meanwhile, conspirators, criminals, and other assorted bad actors have figured out how to use social media sites to promote bogus messages, leveraging a new information ecosystem based on bias and siloed beliefs rather than expertise, credibility, and the common ground (Crovitz & Moran, 2020). How can teachers respond to this new reality?

Since the consumption of digital media and "news" (of varying truth) seems inevitable, it's essential that students learn how to analyze and create such texts themselves to understand how they work—in a sense, to "play" with these genres purposefully so they don't "get played." Reading an online post in which a politician lies is one thing, but actually *creating* digital texts that manipulate meaning helps students understand the dimensions of rhetorical impact and influence. As scholar Renee Hobbs (2020) points out in *Mind Over Media: Propaganda for a Digital Age*, creating multiple kinds of digital content "prepares students for life in a democratic society because [it] is a major way that people try to influence public opinion and make social change" (p. 5).

Students spend a significant amount of their time consuming (and often creating) digital media.[1] Understanding rhetoric[2] in digital spaces can help them become savvier users and consumers of the language that they already embrace. A rhetorical approach to grammar instruction, using digital tools in digital spaces, teaches students to create language for a purposeful effect (Crovitz & Devereaux, 2017). Grammar instruction is best understood and most meaningful when it is embedded as an authentic part of writing instruction and language study (Ferdig et al., 2014). And since many of our students already write in digital spaces, learning the rules of grammar and language through digital contexts can both engage students and equip them with the 21st century skills that they need to be effective communicators.

As we consider ways to teach language in digital spaces, we need to make sure we're all working from the same understanding, so we're going to pause here and clarify our vision. Namely, we would like to see a paradigm shift from *grammar instruction* to *language study*. Let us explain:

1. *Language study* aligns with all levels of the profession, kindergarten through college, and it's right there in how we describe the field: "English language arts."

---

1. See Chapter 2.

2. Rhetoric, in this case, refers to how words are used purposefully to influence people's understandings and beliefs.

2. *Language study* offers a better template to explore the region between a single word and a larger passage. Studying the *language* of a sentence (or a line, stanza, or paragraph) presumes a specific *user of language* (a writer, speaker, or composer) and thus a specific rhetorical situation. With its morass of rules and conventions, grammar as a conventional classroom focus often leads in the opposite direction: toward a realm of abstract, supposed truths (where the author's intentions and options are minimized or ignored) rather than contextual fit.
3. A *language study* approach invites us to view privileged dialects such as Standard American English or Academic English as a form of *foreign language* … which they are since no one is raised as a native speaker of either one. The power these dialects possess is socially granted rather than inherent, and a language study approach can expose assumptions of morality and privilege to help students crack these useful codes.
4. Starting from a linguistic perspective (rather than the often-alienating nomenclature of grammar) acknowledges students themselves as legitimate *experts with language* in their own right

(Devereaux & Crovitz, 2018, pp. 19–20)

When we study specific grammar concepts under the umbrella of *language study*, we gain multiple benefits in the classroom: we honor the knowledge and skills our students possess in digital spaces; we can show students how people purposefully use language in these spaces to manipulate, market, and mediate products and beliefs; and, finally, we can help students become savvy consumers and creators of digital content.

TEN IDEAS FOR USING DIGITAL TOOLS TO TEACH RHETORICAL GRAMMAR

In the sections that follow, we provide ideas for teaching rhetorical grammar through digital technology. We don't expect you to add more to your curriculum—we all know that's impractical. Everyone reading this book already has a full curriculum. Instead, we like the idea of integration.[3] What does this mean? First, we can consider how certain grammatical concepts support the themes in our existing units. For example, later in this chapter, we discuss how passive voice can help people dodge or avoid blame. When integrating instruction, we think of where the idea of "dodging or avoiding blame" complements the theme, texts, and/or writing we are already teaching. We might envision a discussion involving passive voice working well in a unit with novels such as *All American Boys, To Kill a Mockingbird,* or *The Hunger Games* series. Importantly, we don't advocate for covering more than one or two grammatical concepts per unit. Mastery takes time and practice, and when we try to teach three, four, or five grammatical concepts in one unit, no one is learning anything. By limiting the number of concepts, we open time for grammar as language study—rhetorical explorations of context and purpose.[4]

---

3. For a deeper discussion of how to integrate grammar concepts purposefully into thematic units, see *More Grammar to Get Things Done* (Crovitz & Devereaux, 2019).
4. This is not to say that you wouldn't have mini-lessons throughout the year, refreshing and supporting student knowledge and practice.

We do not believe that grammar instruction should occupy an entire class period in most cases—or appear as drudgery through a decontextualized lesson ("Today we are going to learn about commas! Tomorrow we will learn about gerunds!"). Instead, grammar instruction should help students become better readers, writers, thinkers, and communicators (which stand-alone grammar exercises don't do). So while we offer overviews of grammar definitions below as well as examples of digital tools in the classroom, we also want to emphasize that these ideas are forays into larger discussions of how language works in our digital world(s)—an idea we dig into deeply in Chapters 4 and 5.

As we're talking about language and rhetorical grammar instruction, we'd like to also consider National Council of Teachers of English's (NCTE) *Beliefs for Integrating Technology into the English Language Arts Classroom* position statement (NCTE, 2018).[5] This document leans on four principles for using technology of any kind in the ELA classroom (with our thoughts in italics below):

1. Literacy means literacies.
   In other words, there are many different ways to demonstrate literacy, not just through print-based forms and skills.
2. Consider literacies before technologies.
   Meaning that the technology should not necessarily drive instruction—building literacies should.
3. Technologies provide new ways to consume and produce texts.
   This one seems obvious.
4. Technologies and their associated literacies are not neutral.
   So true. Issues of power—who has it, who decides what counts, whose voices are heard—underlie all language use.

Technology is sometimes viewed as simply a tool to do a familiar communicative task in a different format or context. But technology also has the possibility to transform us in ways we perhaps don't anticipate. How we think, see ourselves, express ideas, exist within, and make sense of the world—all of this and more can be shaped by the affordances and constraints of the digital (Jones & Hafner, 2021). We often tell our preservice teachers that "content comes first," regardless of mode—in essence, that the meaning of our communication is what's most important, not the tool we're using. The reality, however, is more complicated, as sometimes the tool transforms what we can say and how we say it.[6]

Although it is likely that some of the digital tech we mention in this section will have become irrelevant or passé (hello, MySpace) shortly after publication of this book, we have tried to provide an overview of the *types* of digital tools that could help students practice rhetorical moves. We will provide some names, but it is our hope that you may already know of some specific websites or tools that would be perfect for the job.

Lastly, we want to reassure you that we have tried and tested all of these ideas with actual students. Some of these ideas were created and tweaked through grammar courses

---

5. Read the full position statement here: https://ncte.org/statement/beliefs-technology-preparation-english-teachers.
6. Think of Twitter, for example, which allows only a certain number of characters; or TikTok, which just increased the max length of their videos from one to three minutes; or Instagram, where you combine words with texts to share meaning. These tools affect what we can say and how we can say it—in other words, they affect meaning.

we taught to preservice teachers, while others were used with secondary students—both by us and by our teacher colleagues. Like a great recipe, these ideas are best when you add your own flair to them. We do not want to prescribe a fixed way of teaching, rather, we advocate for you to make these ideas your own, tailored to your own students and curricular needs.

SENTENCES AND NONSENTENCES THROUGH DIGITAL STICKY NOTES

When considering grammar in digital spaces, the sentence is an interesting place to begin. Although the traditional definition of a sentence may be "a noun and a verb," this does not account for the types of sentences we use in everyday speech, such as "Wow" or "Git!" (Crovitz & Devereaux, 2017, p. 52). In our definition of sentences, we draw on the concept of a "complete thought." This seems to cover the bases for those sentences that are one word or that do not adhere to the traditional definition of noun and verb.

With this understanding, then, we can say that a "nonsentence" is a phrase, clause, or group of words that don't make sense in context. For example, complete sentences (or complete thoughts) about someone's new shoes might be "Wow!" or "Cool new kicks!" Yet, a nonsentence might be "Because they were made by Nike." This doesn't make any sense because it isn't a complete thought. (It is worth noting, however, that this might be a perfectly acceptable response to the question "Why did you buy those?" So, context does matter.)

In secondary ELA classrooms, we often focus on paragraph structure and essay types,[7] leaving the basics of sentence creation to the elementary folks. However, sentences matter. We tell students to "vary their sentence structure," but how often do we provide spaces for students to focus on just one sentence—to play with it and to see how simple changes affect the impact and the scope of the surrounding context? To help students explore sentence construction, we like using digital sticky notes. Sticky notes help students move things around, encouraging students to play with words and to understand that word order is not "locked in." For this activity, you could begin using sentences in mentor texts (or, better yet, sentences of your own), but it is ideal to move to student-created sentences for this exercise.[8]

As far as a specific post-it note tool for this activity, Hyler and Hicks (2017) recommend using Linoit.it. We have found that Google Jamboard is fantastic for whole-class collaboration in real time. Or, in a pinch, you can use the sticky notes app that comes on a laptop computer (both Apple and Microsoft). Whatever specific tool you choose, the point is to play around with sentences, and using colorful, sticky note-type images can help students learn a purposeful digital tool.

---

7. Although this isn't a book about writing instruction, we do think it worth mentioning here that professional writers never sit down and think "okay, now I'm going to write a persuasive essay." Professional writers integrate different styles, genres, and tools to create a powerful essay—a little narrative, a little expository, a little persuasive, etc.

8. As another note, if you are bound by standards and standardized tests to teach the four types of sentences (declarative, interrogative, imperative, and exclamatory), this is a good activity to help students understand the differences between those types of sentences. However, we do not advocate teaching "types of sentences" unless you are bound. Again, in the real world, no one knows this terminology or really cares.

Why Teach This?

In this exercise, we see our students playing with language and colorful sticky notes as if they were Lego building blocks—a metaphor that helps students understand that the words and phrases within sentences can move, a concept not often supported or even introduced in traditional grammar workbooks. We ask students to explain their choices so that they can think through the impact of the changes and whether those changes also affect the larger context. For example, in Figure 3.1, we asked students to consider different types of sentences,[9] and how changing the types of sentences in the passage changes the meaning of the passage.

In this example, you can see the student chose a passage from a Harry Potter novel to dissect. The original passage contains fragments and questions, helping to underscore Harry's confused mental state about being chosen to attend Hogwarts. The student decided to change the passage's original rhetorical effect and make Harry more confident. She felt that her rewritten sentence came across as having "more emotion." She used sticky notes in Google Jamboard to dissect the sentence, rewrite it, and then explain her choices.[10] Below are directions that you can photocopy or re-type and hand out to your students as they complete this activity.

Student Handout: Sentences and Sticky Notes

1. Open Google Jamboard (or other sticky note site) on an internet-enabled device.
2. Choose a mentor sentence from a text or a sentence from your own writing. Type it out on a single sticky note on the site. (For example, write the sentence onto a yellow sticky.)
3. On a separate sticky note, rewrite the sentence, playing around with wording and phrasing.
4. On a third sticky note, change the sentence into a nonsentence.[11]
5. Finally, using the Text feature, write a note to explain your rhetorical choices. Why did you change the sentence as you did? Do you think the new sentence is better or worse than the first? Did the sentence's meaning change through the revisions you made? How so?

CLAUSES THROUGH MEMES

Digital memes—image and text combinations that use common templates to make a humorous point—are now a ubiquitous part of online media culture. Biologist Richard Dawkins coined the term "meme" in his 1977 book *The Selfish Gene* in an effort to describe social or cultural phenomena that behave like genes in their ability to replicate

---

9. Here, we are referring to declarative, imperative, interrogative, and exclamatory types of sentences.
10. The student example shows revisions with a small passage; however, the student directions focus on one sentence. We believe that work with one sentence is a valuable place to begin, but if you feel your students can address an entire passage, feel free to do so.
11. Again, if you are bound to teach types of sentences, here you might change sentences from declarative to interrogative or exclamatory.

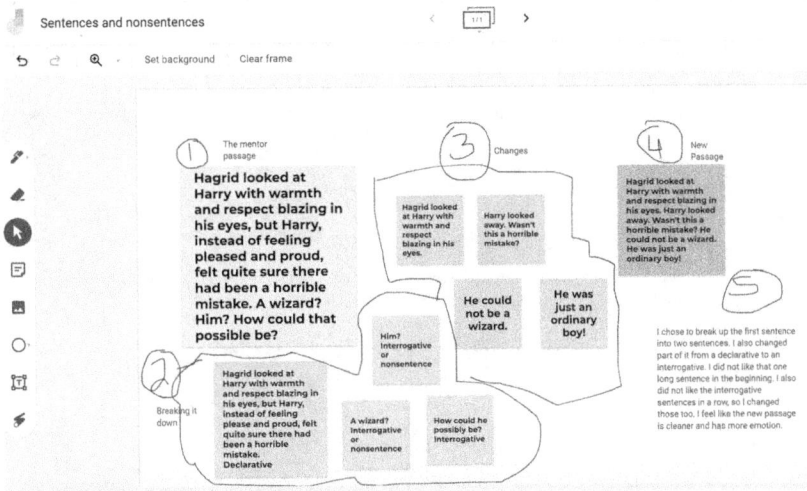

Figure 3.1 Digital Sticky Notes on Google Jamboard

through human communication. Common examples of memes include idioms and sayings (e.g., "an apple a day keeps the doctor away"), gestures (e.g., the "OK" hand signal), gender-specific clothing (e.g., neckties for men), fables, jokes, common advice, or any piece of cultural information easily propagated. As with genes, Dawkins proposed that memes can die out or evolve, shedding associations and taking on new meanings (Crovitz & Moran, 2020, p. 63).

Meme messages now saturate popular culture, and your students will no doubt be very familiar with such texts. Communicating through digital memes condenses a message into a short and memorable visual form, and just about every meme template follows particular rules of usage and convention. The classic Success Kid meme, for example, follows a specific formula (see Figure 3.2). The top phrase (typically beginning with a past tense verb) captures a challenging or troublesome moment, with the bottom phrase acting as a rejoinder of triumph (or, well, success), epitomized by the image of the toddler in a fist-pump pose.

Figure 3.2 Success Kid Meme Examples

1S AND 0S: THE DIGITAL NUTS AND BOLTS   29

Figure 3.3 Bad Luck Brian Meme Examples

The Bad Luck Brian meme (Figure 3.3) follows a similar structure, but this time the pattern is reversed. Here, the top statement (with its present tense verb phrasing) highlights an earnest or successful initial action only to be ironically countered by the born-loser humor to follow in the second line. Brian's goofball expression and sweater vest style unites the meme as a playful multimodal mockery of hapless dorks everywhere.

Other templates rely on an understood punchline or background knowledge for humor, such as the familiar "One does not simply" meme featuring Boromir (actor Sean Bean) from Peter Jackson's *Lord of the Rings* films. This meme references Boromir's frustration with the idea of a single person hiking into Mordor in order to destroy the One Ring.[12] As a meme, his remark is repurposed comedically to illustrate the enormous difficulty or frustration involved with particular actions (as in Figure 3.4).

Likewise, the familiar "Hey Girl" meme draws upon heartthrob actor Ryan Gosling as the epitome of a handsome, romantic partner (Figure 3.5). With this meme, the humor lies in the hyperbole of Gosling's next-level attributes as the ideal man.

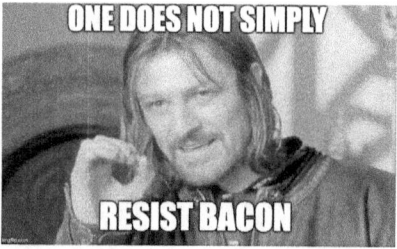 

Figure 3.4 Typical "One Does Not Simply" Memes

---

12. As Boromir puts it in *The Fellowship of the Ring*, "one does not simply walk into Mordor."

Figure 3.5 A Typical "Hey Girl" Meme

Practicing with meme analysis and creation—studying how to make something funny with words and a picture, basically—means noticing linguistic patterns and meeting usage expectations. When we create such a meme, we use the language conventions of a genre to accomplish a real communication goal. That is, we use grammatical knowledge to achieve a rhetorical purpose. In the examples above, students need mastery of phrases and parallelism[13] (among other understandings) to make the jokes work. Importantly, they'll often need an understanding of how irony produces humor. As students tend to struggle with irony and its application, a quick refresher on the concept is a good idea since it's a common element in meme humor. While most students understand how to read memes intuitively, they may need explicit instruction on these conventions.

Okay. Now that we have the basics of meme creation, what grammar concepts might we teach with memes? Grammatically, memes can be useful vehicles for studying both independent and dependent clauses (see below for a refresher of what independent and dependent clauses are).

---

13. Quick reminder: Parallelism means that your choice of wording is balanced. For example, the sentence *She loves running, hiking, and to swim* isn't parallel because that last item in the list ("to swim") doesn't match the form of the first two with their *-ing* endings. Parallel options could be *She loves running, hiking, and swimming* or *She loves to run, to hike, and to swim.*

> **QUICK REFRESHER: INDEPENDENT AND DEPENDENT CLAUSES**
>
> **Independent:** Independent clauses are a complete thought and can stand alone as sentences, e.g., *She hated getting up early for class.*
>
> **Dependent:** Dependent (or subordinate) clauses contain three language components, a subject, a verb, and a subordinating word[14] (such as *after, when, before, while, because*, etc.). Dependent clauses can't stand on their own as formal sentences.
>
> Consider this sentence: *She hated getting up early for class because she worked late.* In this example, "because she worked late" is the dependent clause. It contains a subordinating word (because), a subject (she), and a verb (worked). Dependent clauses can also contain other words or phrases as well.[15]

Dependent clauses (formed with a subordinating word, subject, and verb) can make rhetorical sense as nonsentences,[16] particularly in dialogue. Used in memes, dependent clauses often act as the explicit "set up" for the humor conveyed. Look at the examples of the "When you realize"[17] meme (see Figure 3.6), in which the image serves to convey the emotional state of a described situation.

What's going on grammatically with these memes? Here's the formula:

meme text [dependent clause] + image [implied independent clause][18] *= complex sentence*

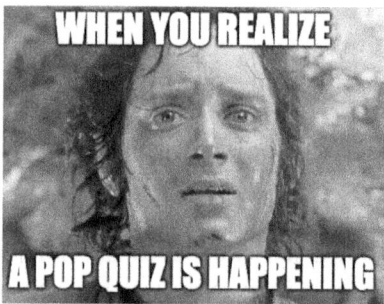 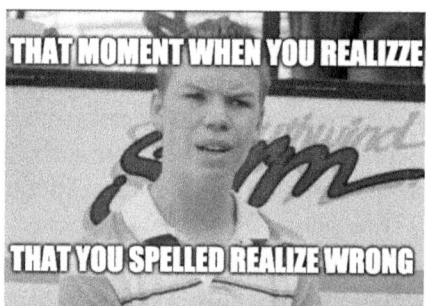

Figure 3.6 "When You Realize" Meme Examples

---

14. In most adverbial clauses, the subordinating word and subject are two separate words, as in "because she loves to swim"; however, in adjectival dependent clauses, the subordinate word and subject can be the same word as in "that is blue." However, this is the type of trivia (and headache) we never encourage teaching.
15. For a deep dive into sentences, nonsentences, and dependent clauses, check out *Grammar to Get Things Done* by Darren Crovitz and Michelle D. Devereaux.
16. See the earlier discussion of sentences and nonsentences with digital sticky notes.
17. And its alternate forms; "that moment when you realize" and "that moment you realize."
18. In these memes, the image functions as an independent clause emphasizing an emotional state: "You're scared," "You're confused," "I'm annoyed," etc. The meme text, meanwhile, functions as the adverbial dependent clause that sets up that emotional punchline.

Figure 3.7 Meme With a Dependent Clause

With the Frodo example on the left, we thus get

When you realize a pop quiz is happening, [you feel immediate terror and anxiety.]

When students understand that any image conveying an emotion or specific circumstance can potentially serve as an implied independent clause, they can experiment with dependent clause overlays to create humor. Subordinating words offer lots of possibilities for perspective and commentary, and your students will quickly stretch toward other variations, as in Figure 3.7.

Experimenting with various textual options over the same image helps show how meaning can shift dramatically. The meme text in Figure 3.7 conveys a kind of diligent-student annoyance (*"I can't focus because you keep whispering!"*), a meaning which can be transformed with alternate text, as in "when the teacher is reminded to assign homework on Friday." Such work can help students grasp how meme images act as "floating signifiers" to promote almost any kind of message—a key facet of visual and media literacy.

To further connect these grammatical moves to real-world concerns, students might list some of their everyday struggles, frustrations, and triumphs, and then use dependent clauses over a particular image to create a meme expressing this experience. Imagine how the pairing of "before you meet your homeroom teacher" and "after you meet your homeroom teacher" might communicate multiple experiences depending on the images used. In the same fashion, students can also take a stance on broader social issues from remote learning to protest movements. Memes are a powerful form of communication, and students can leverage their humorous appeal to make serious statements.

Why Teach This?

Using clauses and memes together helps students understand grammatical implications at work in real-world situations. Most students already have a familiarity with memes, creating and sharing their own versions. However, most probably do not consider the rhetorical impact of the meme or pause to consider the interplay between the image and the words. Practicing meme creation and taking the time to dissect and to discuss how and why these texts work (or don't work) means practicing a dimension of digital literacy that extends to other texts on their social media feeds. Students may gain a greater understanding of the impact of clauses to shape meaning and thus affect how others see the world.

Online meme generators (a Google search away) make this creative work fairly easy, and meme creation apps such as Mematic, Memefactory, and Memedroid are available for mobile devices. Of course, not all meme forms are suitable for the classroom. Search for "clean memes," paying particular attention to how grammatical structures are necessary for communicating humor, irony, and perspective.

> ### Student Handout: Memes and Clauses
> 1. Open an online meme generator site or app on an internet-enabled device.
> 2. Choose an image suitable for your message. Remember that the image acts as the independent clause in your statement.
> 3. Following the prompts on the site for meme creation, craft a dependent clause to go with the image.
> 4. Make sure your text choices work with the implications of the image for a certain purpose: humor, irony, cultural commentary, and so on.
> 5. Write a short reflection paragraph to explain your rhetorical choices.

LEXICAL CATEGORIES THROUGH ANIMATION

Lexical categories, or "parts of speech," are often touted as the bread and butter of grammar instruction. Most of us, as teachers, can easily identify how a word is functioning in context, and we may often coach our students in identifying them as well. However, research has shown us that identification alone doesn't improve students' reading or writing (Hillocks, 1986)—students need opportunities to explore how lexical categories work rhetorically.

Linguists separate lexical categories into open classes (*noun, verb, adjective, adverb*) and closed classes (*preposition, pronoun, conjunction, article*). Open classes change often in our language. When we think of new words, they're almost always going to be a noun, verb, adjective, or adverb. Think of "Jabberwocky" for example—Lewis Carroll made up nouns, verbs, and adjectives—complete nonsense words that make sense in context. However, Carroll didn't mess with the closed class words because the poem wouldn't have made sense. Closed class words are our direction-givers, and when reading, we need all the directions we can get. Not surprisingly, closed class words *don't change* very often in our history. If you look at *Sir Gawain and the Green Knight*, written in the 1300s, you *may* notice some open class words that look familiar, but it's the closed class words that are spelled exactly the same, 700 years later.

For this activity, we recommend focusing on an open class category because those are the most useful to students.[19] Here, we will walk through the activity using *nouns*.

---

19. Strong nouns and verbs make for strong writing, so any chance we have for students to play with these concepts, we embrace it.

As we're sure you've heard, nouns are defined as "people, places, and things"; however, somewhere along the way, "ideas" got added to the definition, and for good reason. "People, places, and things" is a limited definition, and even the addition of "ideas" doesn't capture all of what nouns can be. Linguists Curzan & Adams (2012) remind us that nouns are also concepts (*education*), activities (*studying*), states (*confusion*), and time (*yesterday*). So how then can we best help students understand "noun-ness"?

What if, instead of old and incomplete definitions, we focused on how nouns function in context? Then we could open a space to discuss rhetorical impact and choice, an important component of language study. Nouns follow a couple of easy rules that are unique to this lexical category: (1) they can be made plural or possessive, and (2) they can follow an article. No other lexical category can be made plural or possessive or can follow an article.[20] Simply playing around with these two rules can show students how to identify nouns, though identification is not the end goal. Rhetorical understanding is.

So, what do nouns *do*? Nouns are powerful because they *name*. They name people and places and things and (oh, wait), also states and activities and … You get the point. And the one who names is typically the one who has the power (at least at that particular moment). For this activity, we recommend asking students to choose one recent moment in their online worlds—a new video game, a new viral video (school-appropriate, of course), an artist's hot new release—and search how different sites, influencers, and companies are using *nouns* to describe that moment. (Perhaps, by chance, you have students who aren't as tuned in online. They can always choose a recent moment in the news for analysis.) Students can then consider how different nouns are used in different contexts and why particular entities would use particular nouns to describe the latest thing.

To help students understand nouns and how they function in context, we've had success with asking them to create a rhetorical analysis of nouns through animation videos. There are many animation-creation websites and tools, but our favorite is Powtoon. Powtoon has been around since 2012, so our hope is that it will not be obsolete when you are reading this book. There are other animation sites, including the app Toontastic and the website GoAnimate. No doubt others will crop up.

The idea for this activity is based on the principles of reciprocal teaching (Palincsar & Brown, 1984). This theory posits that students will understand a complex task better when they teach it to peers. The principles of reciprocal teaching include a series of overlapping activities that help train students to ask questions as they teach their peers. In the process, they learn more and are more engaged. We used this basic idea to ask students to create animation videos about a lexical category, answering questions such as "how is this lexical category used in these digital spaces" and "to what effect?"

Once the videos are complete, you can host a Rhetorical Film Festival where students provide a quick explanation prior to showing their finished product. The constraints of Powtoon limit videos to one minute long, and some students have found this frustrating. However, this time limit forces them to keep their explanations concise, and it allows all videos from an entire class to be viewed in one day.

---

20. Technically, adjectives and adverbs can follow articles, but those adjectives and adverbs are modifying the nouns that the article is intended for (e.g., **The thoroughly hilarious professor** writes grammar books.)

Why Teach This?

Likely, few of your students are planning to become editors, writers, or English teachers. However, helping students understand the rhetorical impact of nouns and other lexical categories empower your students to become more critical readers, writers, thinkers, and communicators. And when they become the expert on a topic, and then teach the class what they have found, they take ownership over their understanding of the world.

Student Handout: Lexical Categories and Animation

1. Choose a recent moment in your online world (a new video game, a viral video, an artist's new release) and find different people/groups reporting and discussing that moment (influencers, critics, users, companies). Focus on the nouns used to describe this recent moment. Make sure to cite different nouns from different sites.
2. Analyze why different sites would use different nouns. You can consider the following questions:
    a. How do the nouns differ?
    b. Do some sites use nouns that are positive and others use nouns that are negative? Why would this happen?
    c. Why does each site use the noun it does? What is that particular site selling and/or supporting?
3. After you have organized your analysis, log into the animation site or app using an internet-enabled device.
4. Following the templates in the site, make a short, one-minute video that teaches your classmates about the rhetorical findings surrounding the online moment.
5. Be creative in your use of color and words. Use all the affordances of the site to help jazz up your explanation of this lexical category.
6. Share the completed video with the class. Be prepared to explain your choices.

CONJUNCTIONS THROUGH FACEBOOK OR INSTAGRAM

To help students use conjunctions with rhetorical purpose, we turn to social media. Social media sites have their own specific functions, and many of your students are well versed in the nuances of each. Some students are avid consumers and creators of social media content, using the various platforms to build identities, negotiate relationships, remix other media, or read for information (Hicks, 2013). Others are happy to just sit on the sidelines and occasionally read or post. Students' involvement in social media runs the gamut from "hanging out" (i.e., surfing, casual reading, and occasional posting) to "messing around" (i.e., involvement in online games informally, as well as other sites) to "geeking out" (i.e., full participants in gaming sites and/or creators of digital content) (Ito et al., 2009). These various statuses are fluid and can change, but we are confident that the vast majority of our students have some kind of online presence.

Popular social media sites (currently) include TikTok, Snapchat, Facebook, and Instagram. For this particular activity, we focus on Facebook or Instagram since they include still images with text. As you likely know, Facebook is available online and on mobile devices, while Instagram is app-based and intended for use on phones. The primary function of Facebook is to share written content, links, and pictures, while the primary function of Instagram is to share photos with some written content. Posts on Facebook tend to be more language-driven, while posts on Instagram are more visually oriented. We think both have their place in the classroom and can be used to practice a wide variety of rhetorical strategies and communication skills. When choosing a site for this activity, consider your students' fluency around discussing rhetorical choices and impact. Perhaps your students need to focus on the choices made in one sentence (Instagram) or your students are ready to explore rhetorical impacts within a larger paragraph (Facebook).

To avoid conflicts with their carefully crafted online identities, we do not ask students to post directly to their own sites or walls. Instead, we create a classroom Facebook page or Instagram handle and have students post there. That way, they can keep their in-school and out-of-school identities separate. Additionally, we would like to highlight here that students need to use the real website, either Facebook or Instagram, for their in-school activities, rather than a simulated one or a paper handout made to look like one of these sites. The stakes are much higher when students realize that they are posting online, and the affordances of the site will allow others in the classroom—or school—to "like" their post or comment on it. Creating a class Facebook or Instagram page is easy and does not compromise students' privacy as long as they join the page with an alias or alternate name. Furthermore, allowing students to experiment with the actual genre of social media encourages creativity (Gee, 2017).

So now, to conjunctions. It's true—students will walk into your classroom familiar with conjunctions and use them in their writing without a second thought. However, this familiarity is part of what makes conjunctions an appropriate foray into rhetorical grammar instruction: students' confidence can translate to playful experimentation and discussion of rhetorical impacts in digital spaces.

For example, your students are likely very familiar with the most common conjunctions: *and, but, or, so*. However, the lesser-used conjunctions—*for, yet,* and *nor*—can make for interesting rhetorical conversations. How does using *yet* instead of *but* change the tone of an online post (as in "yet she persisted")? Why would a person choose one over the other? What happens to the tone of a post in each case?[21] These types of questions also open spaces to consider online identity and community and how language use denotes in-group or out-group status.[22] For this type of detailed analysis of word choice, we recommend using Instagram since the text in those posts are typically shorter than Facebook.

In addition to Facebook or Instagram, students can use images or memes to demonstrate their understanding of these language options in practice. Depending on the rhetorical situation, using a more formal or less common conjunction choice such as *yet* or *nor* can be effective … or might just come across as pompous and pretentious

---

21. As is probably clear, *nor* and *yet* are less common and more formal than other conjunction options.

22. See Chapter 2 for a more thorough conversation of online identity and community.

Figure 3.8 Contextual Use Of "Nor"

(see Figure 3.8). How can your students show what they know about conjunction appropriateness in specific situations through visual texts? These kinds of activities, like those with absolutes and participial phrases (discussed later in this chapter), open a space to discuss how text and image can work together in digital spaces to create new meanings.

Another option with conjunctions and social media is questioning an old conjunction rule of yore: "never begin a sentence with a conjunction." But experienced writers use this rhetorical move all the time to control rhythm or emphasize a point. Playing around with breaking this rule might work best with a larger passage, which means Facebook might be a better choice. Starting a sentence with a well-chosen coordinating conjunction can be an effective way to conclude a short passage, for instance.

Why Teach This?

As we mentioned above, students are already familiar with coordinating conjunctions, meaning it's a place where they can move to rhetorical uses with some confidence. These activities also give students an opportunity to further explore how image and text work together in digital spaces to create new meanings.

> ***Student Handout: Conjunctions and Social Media***
>
> 1. Navigate to the teacher-created Instagram page on your internet-enabled device and log in.
> 2. Create a post with a sentence that uses a conjunction.
> 3. Create a second post using the same sentence, but this time use a *different* conjunction (possible pairs might include or/nor, but/yet, and/so, etc.). Notice how the change in conjunction shifts the tone and meaning of the sentence.
> 4. Next, locate an appropriate image for each sentence version. The image should illustrate the tone and meaning of the text it accompanies.
> 5. Be ready to explain how each image relates to the tone of each sentence.

ABSOLUTES AND PARTICIPIAL PHRASES THROUGH DIGITAL SLIDESHOWS

As Crovitz and Devereaux (2019) note in *More Grammar to Get Things Done*, teaching absolute phrases and participial phrases together makes good sense—even though the two grammar concepts do not always have the same function. When boiled down to their essence, both phrases illuminate an idea found in the complete sentence they accompany. Here's a quick refresher of the two concepts.

QUICK REFRESHER: PARTICIPIAL PHRASES AND ABSOLUTES

Participial phrase: a phrase with an *-ing*, *-ed*, or *-en* verbal that acts like an adjective. (Example: *Overflowing with pepperoni and cheese*, the pizza looked like a work of art. The phrase "overflowing with pepperoni and cheese" modifies the word "pizza," so it acts as an adjective.)

Absolute phrase: The most basic definition (and one we advocate that is the focus of your instruction) of an absolute is *a noun + participle (+ any modifying words/ phrase)*. The main difference between an absolute phrase and a participial phrase is that an absolute has a noun before the participle in the phrase. (Example: *Eyes brimming with tears*, the quarterback accepted the high school's MVP trophy. The phrase "eyes brimming with tears" is the absolute phrase. It also has the noun [eyes] before the participle [brimming].)

Here are a couple of more examples for good measure—because these phrases can be difficult:
- *Snapping the skateboard in half over her knee*, Latisha swore she would never try a kickflip again. (Participial phrase containing the participle "snapping" modifies the subject "Latisha.")
- *Hands trembling as he spoke*, Anthony asked his English teacher for an extension on the paper. (Absolute phrase with the noun "hands" before the participle "trembling" modifies the entire rest of the sentence.)

To help students master these concepts, we've used digital slideshows. There are a wide variety of slideshow platforms available, and students find them an easy and interesting tool for creation. The most familiar platform may be PowerPoint, but our students also like Google Slides, VoiceThread, Flipsnack, Adobe Spark, and Pear Deck. We advocate for free digital tools as we don't want our students (or us) to pay for a digital tool for one assignment. For this particular activity, we like to use VoiceThread, as students can upload images and text and then record an explanation of their rhetorical choices.

Obviously, digital slideshows aren't new; students have been creating such presentations for years. The emphasis here is on students using the presentation mode—and the opportunity for an audience—in order to manipulate language to create digital stories that communicate powerful feelings. Typical PowerPoint "presentations" often end up with students simply reading aloud onscreen text as they advance slides, which rarely makes for a compelling experience. Voiceover narration, meanwhile, is a powerful element of many digital texts (as millions of TikTok and YouTube videos demonstrate). We want students to practice and employ this digital affordance.

The final slides of the show might be students discussing the rhetorical impact of the additions and changes they made to their piece. This work also encourages collaboration and discussion about the rhetorical impact of absolutes and participial phrases.

We start this activity by asking students to respond to a prompt such as, "Tell about the most thrilling adventure you have experienced." Some retell daring tales of climbing water towers or sneaking out of the house, while others write about family vacations. Regardless of topic, we encourage a short response, no longer than a paragraph or two at the most.[23]

Once students have drafted a response, we ask them to work in groups, sharing their narratives. Peers listen to stories twice, once to understand the piece and a second time with an ear towards detail and impact—what's effective, and where do they think the author can *illuminate* moments in their stories more purposefully? Students revise their narratives with the goal of including appropriate absolute and participial phrases that emphasize particular moments.[24]

For the digital component of this assignment, students choose images to illustrate their narrative and act as accompanying text; one image per sentence might be a good starting point.[25] Importantly, students should be able to explain the reasoning behind their decisions. Sometimes the thinking can be obvious: we're all used to using images that align with or complement existing text-based meaning in order to amplify or illustrate (as in Figures 3.9 and 3.10). But sometimes—often for purposes of humor or

Figure 3.9 Participial Phrase With Image

---

23. When asking students to consider rhetorical choices and meanings, small chunks of text are far easier to manipulate than longer pieces.
24. We've had success with discussing *sentence combining* with absolutes and participles. Neighboring sentences can often be combined to create tighter prose.
25. An important benefit of using one image per sentence, and making sure students can justify their choice of image, is that they may realize they have superfluous sentences and information. It encourages yet another level of rewriting.

Figure 3.10 Absolute Phrase With Image

commentary, or just to tell a new story—divergent meanings are what we intend, as in Figure 3.11 (Jones & Hafner, 2021). When we juxtapose images with text or narration, new meanings become possible.

Why Teach This?

We are firm believers that when students can identify and justify their choices, they grow as writers and thinkers. This activity emphasizes the purpose behind specific choices and the potential impact of those choices on others.

Figure 3.11 Divergent Image and Text Combination

> **Student Handout: Participial Phrases and Absolutes Through Digital Slide Shows**
>
> 1. In your journal, respond to the following prompt: What is the most thrilling adventure you have experienced? Use sensory language to describe how it felt, appeared, and sounded. This response should be no longer than one or two paragraphs.
> 2. Share your response with your group twice. Listen once to understand the story, and then a second time for how the story is told. Where might changes be needed to increase drama or tension?
> 3. Individually, edit your narrative, adding participial and absolute phrases and combining sentences. As you make these choices, consider how these changes impact your story. Are the moments described clearer? Is your intended effect more visceral?
> 4. After editing your narrative, get back into your groups and reread your narratives. Solicit advice from your peers, and if you believe their advice works for your piece, make final edits.
> 5. On an internet-enabled device, locate images for your slideshow, aiming for about one image per sentence. Keep in mind that your image choices carry rhetorical implications as well. The pictures you choose might align with and illuminate the meaning of your sentences. (Depending on your intent, the images can also complicate or diverge from textual meaning as well.)
> 6. Add these images into a slideshow program, such as PowerPoint, Google Slides, or VoiceThread.
> 7. Pair one sentence from your narrative with each image. Be sure to adjust the text so that it does not block any key elements in the image.
> 8. Arrange the images with sentences in an order that makes sense to you.
> 9. Record a voiceover.
> 10. On a final slide, explain several of the rhetorical choices you made to your piece. For instance, you might discuss your intention in pairing specific images with certain text.[26]
> 11. Share your digital narrative with the class (or in groups).

ADJECTIVAL PHRASES THROUGH VIRTUAL REALITY

Adjectives are a deceptively nuanced concept for young writers to tackle. On the surface, descriptive words and phrases—*small, pretty, very happy, sorta hungry*—are some of the most basic language elements and easy for most children to use in practical ways. Complexity emerges, however, in figuring out *which* adjectival concepts to emphasize, along with how many and for what purpose. A long train of adjectives ("my old, big, thick,

---

[26]. You may find that this rhetorical discussion of each slide is too much. If so, have students choose one image and sentence to rhetorically analyze at the end of the presentation.

Table 3.1 Different Contexts, Different Words

Context, Purpose, or Focus	Blanket Attributes Worth Emphasizing
Winter is approaching…	warmth, size, fabric
Grandma made it…	homemade quality, fabric, durability, history
We're going to watch the big game!	size, design, warmth, personal history, affiliation
My personal, eclectic style…	design, pattern, fabric, how it matches (or doesn't) other items in the room
My need to relax after a tough day…	warmth, comfort, softness, familiarity

plaid, wool, handmade, lucky New York Jets blanket is so warm, soft, cozy, and comfy in winter") is rarely an effective choice.[27]

Part of the trick with adjectives is their *judicious and specific use*.[28] A blizzard of descriptor words can easily overwhelm an audience and obscure what's really special about the thing being described. Why are we talking about that favorite blanket, anyway? Our purpose matters! Consider how the different contexts in Table 3.1 might affect just what we describe.

Clarifying our intent both *restrains* and *focuses* an adjectival description, ultimately helping a reader's understanding match a writer's vision.

A second productive area to develop adjectival fluency is *amplification*. As with most language work, we can anchor this instruction on what students already know, starting with the word "very." As Table 3.2 demonstrate, some metacognitive work can help students move beyond "very" to precise and evocative descriptions based on specific context.

Discussions of synonyms will be familiar to most students; it's useful to have options for more precise and accurate description. The use of adverb-enhanced adjectival

Table 3.2 Adjectival Phrases for Intentional Amplification

"very" Adjectival Phrase	A Few Adjectival Synonyms	Adverb + Adjective, Determined by Context and Circumstance
very hot	sweltering, scorching	oppressively hot
very bad	terrible, awful	cringingly bad
very yummy	delicious	painfully delicious
very big	enormous, gigantic	awkwardly large
very expensive	costly, overpriced	unreasonably expensive
very good-looking	handsome	strikingly handsome

---

27. Truly, we earnestly argue against teaching simple, strung-together adjectives for description. If you search "writers quotes adjectives," you will find that successful authors often warn against their overuse. However, for this particular section, we think Mark Twain's thoughts on adjectives help our point the most: "When you catch an adjective, kill it. No, I don't mean utterly, but kill most of them—then the rest will be valuable. They weaken when they are close together. They give strength when they are far apart [and, we should add, purposefully employed]."

28. And granted, the same might be said about any language element.

phrases, however, opens new avenues for characterizing different circumstances. We're not just substituting a fancier word in this case but shaping adjectives to help express a particular purpose or perspective. A new house that is *awkwardly large* is way different from one that is *impressively large*. Was that movie *amusingly bad* or *painfully bad*?[29] It all depends on the context and the experience to be conveyed. Is Ryan Gosling *classically handsome*, *strikingly handsome*, or *boyishly handsome*?[30] These kinds of adjectival phrases are quite good at conveying specific visceral descriptions as well as the writer's particular perspective. The "brushstrokes" of grammar, as Noden (2011) calls them, paint a picture that clearly communicates an author's feelings and beliefs. The advertising industry understands the power and value of such phrases: as we know, Lucky Charms are *magically delicious* and Keebler cookies are *uncommonly good*.

QUICK REFRESHER: ADJECTIVAL PHRASES

Adjectival phrase: a group of words that contain a head adjective and modify a noun:
- We enjoyed watching the ***strikingly beautiful*** sun as it set over the ocean. In this sentence, the adjectival phrase is "strikingly beautiful" with "beautiful" as the head adjective.
- My ***incredibly crazy*** dog ran along the water's edge. The adjectival phrase is "incredibly crazy" with "crazy" as the head adjective.[31]

If adjectival phrases help to convey a writer's particular view, then simple virtual reality (VR) devices can help students better understand this purpose. The immersive and interactive nature of VR can be viscerally affecting for students; they often emerge with powerful reactions to the experience that map well onto adjectival phrasing.

Our favorite device is a Google Cardboard, available from Amazon or Google for $10 or less. As the name suggests, these devices are made of stiff cardboard and are quite durable (see Figure 3.12). Students begin by downloading a free VR app for their phones—Sites in VR, Google Arts and Culture, or Within VR are good places to start, though there are many other options. After opening the app, the phone is inserted into the Cardboard, which is then held up to one's eyes to act as a visor-type VR headset.

Users can navigate within the app using the Cardboard controls, choosing from a variety of images for 3D interactions. The virtual experience is fascinating and often uncanny; immersed in this space, one can physically look in all directions—up, to the side, behind—and move through lifelike VR spaces. Reconstructed geographic and historical locations mean that students can explore a reproduction of the Globe Theatre or visit areas around the world.

---

29. For us, *Sharknado* could be described as *amusingly bad* while *Howard the Duck* was just *painfully bad*. You might bring this discussion to the classroom floor; we're sure your students have some opinions.
30. Clearly, it's the last one.
31. The noun is not part of the adjectival phrase. If we included the noun, as in "my incredibly crazy dog," we would be discussing the noun phrase, not the adjectival phrase.

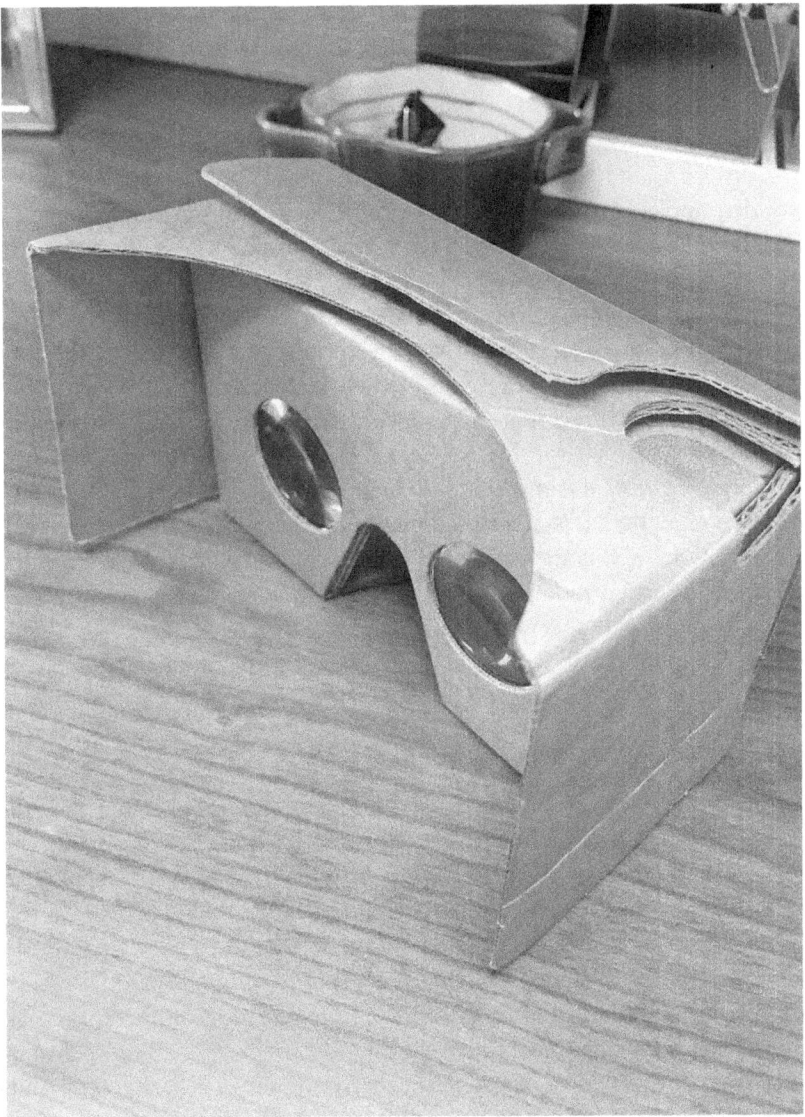

Figure 3.12 A Google Cardboard Virtual Reality Device

Working in pairs, students take turns navigating and exploring the three-dimensional space. The student using the Cardboard describes the experience aloud, while the partner records the details of these observations. Once finished, students create adjectival phrases to describe their visual experience; in doing so, they also try to convey a specific perspective, which may be inflected by emotion, prior experiences, and other distinctly individual elements. Here we would like to emphasize again that students should not be creating a list of adjectives; instead, they should consider the adjectival phrases we discussed above: a purposeful adverb supporting a purposeful adjective.

We've had success with this activity with both middle and high school students (Moran, 2021; Moran & Woodall, 2019). In this work, we paired the writing of adjectival phrases with larger text-centered units. In one iteration, students viewed VR images of the Great Depression while reading *To Kill a Mockingbird* (Lee, 2002/1961); in another, students viewed VR images of Mount Everest as part of a unit featuring *Into Thin Air* (Krakauer, 1997).

Why Teach This?

Our use of descriptive language doesn't happen in a vacuum—instead, our choices reflect our beliefs about and judgments toward the subjects around us. We want our students to practice the rhetorical dimensions of adjectives and adjectival phrases, as these concepts are quite useful for communicating a stance or attitude, be it praise, criticism, respect, or disdain. If you write about "ridiculously overpriced" concert tickets, then we have a good sense of both detail ("they're expensive!") and your attitude ("a ripoff!"). Helping students practice this construct will encourage them to write with passion and confidence.

VR is an excellent vehicle for this activity in that it catapults the viewer into a weirdly representational world that can seem quite real. VR can perhaps generate reactions and emotions more reliably than static two-dimensional images, and generally speaking, it's much easier to write about such personal reactions and feelings when they are recent; interacting with a virtual mountain landscape might trigger a genuine feeling of awe, which can in turn assist the viewer in writing about that feeling with fresh perspective. Rather than relying on recall, writing with VR is akin to painting *en plein air*.[32]

> ***Student Handout: Adjectival Phrases Through VR***
>
> 1. Work with a partner. One of you should use a smartphone, and the other be ready to record descriptions (roles will be reversed later).
> 2. Download a virtual reality app onto your phone.
> 3. Open the app and search for the specific "place" or "thing" you wish to view. For example, your teacher may have instructed you to view the "Restless in Hong Kong" movie short in the Within VR app.
> 4. Once you have navigated to the appropriate selection on the app, insert the phone into a Google Cardboard.
> 5. One student should look through the viewer on the device. Stand up and look above, below, and behind you. Really get inside the image and explore.
> 6. Describe what you are seeing to your partner, who should record your observations. Be as descriptive as you can and be sure to express your feelings and thoughts.
> 7. Switch roles. Allow your partner to view the images through the VR device while you record their descriptions.
> 8. Sorting through your recorded descriptions, create a passage with a few powerful adjectival phrases (the adverb-adjective construction). Remember what Mark Twain says about adjectives: *When you catch an adjective, kill it. No, I don't mean utterly, but kill most of them—then the rest will be valuable. They weaken when they are close together. They give strength when they are far apart.* Make sure your adjectival phrases are strengthening your description!

---

32. i.e., "in plain air," in which an artist's subject is in full view.

9. Your passage should paint an accurate picture of what you experienced but also convey your feeling, emotion, or perspective as well. For instance, phrases such as *shockingly steep*, *terribly poor*, and *surprisingly beautiful* both describe scenes as well as reveal something about one's own reactions.

ACTIVE AND PASSIVE VOICE THROUGH PODCASTS

Our main goal of grammar instruction is that our students become thoughtful creators and consumers of language. We want the rhetorical effects of language to be clear to them, and we want them to feel confident in their power to use specific rhetorical strategies to achieve an effect. Active and passive voice are a good foray into these discussions. Author Stephen King (2010) says in *On Writing: A Memoir of the Craft* that the passive voice implies reservation. He calls it "the timid voice" and advises against using it at all costs. However, we disagree. The passive voice may indeed be timid if you're writing a mystery novel ("Harriet grabbed the knife" versus "The knife was grabbed by Harriet"), but it is quite useful if you want to negotiate power in specific situations.

News outlets frequently use the passive voice when key actors aren't known yet. For example, they may use the sentence "The bank was robbed" when no one has been arrested or accused yet. Likewise, the sentence "A man was killed today in an officer-involved shooting" avoids naming the police officer who shot the man. Passive voice can often be about power—who has it and who wields it. For example, we can consider the old-political standby, "Mistakes were made." Not "I made a mistake" but rather the passive that implies "Someone made a mistake; I'm not saying it was me, but someone made a mistake, but notice that no blame was assigned." This hedging effect of passive voice can be important, so we don't agree with King's (2010) suggestion to never use the passive voice in any situation. Instead, we want students to be savvy users of language, massaging the tense of a sentence or the voice of a passage so that it suits their purposes.

QUICK REFRESHER: ACTIVE AND PASSIVE VOICE

Active voice: A sentence structure that typically employs the subject-verb-object (SVO) pattern. (Example: *My friend loves Justin Bieber.* In this sentence, the subject is "friend," the verb is "loves," and the object is "Justin Bieber.")

Passive voice: A sentence structure in which the subject of the sentence is the recipient of the verb's action. (Example: *Justin Bieber is loved by my friend.*)

So what we shared above are the traditional definitions of active and passive. Maybe that was all you needed. However, those definitions alone never worked for us, so here is a little more.

> There are two truths about passive that make the sentence easier to identify:
> 1. Passive voice has a specific verb construction—a helping verb (or got) with a *past tense* action verb (in the example above, "is loved");
> 2. You can add "by zombies" at the end of passive sentences; sometimes the passive sentence already has a "by" construction at the end (in the example above: "by my friend"), but if you can't find a "by" construction at the end of the sentence, you can add "by zombies" to a passive sentence, and it will make sense.
>
> Here are two more examples:
> - She does not eat Brussels sprouts. (active; subject/verb/object pattern)
> - Brussels sprouts are not eaten by her (passive; you can see the two verbs you need for passive, the helping verb [are] and the past tense action verb [eaten]; also, notice that "by" construction at the end [by her]).

We enjoy using podcasts or voiceover digital platforms to teach students about the shifts of power and responsibility in active and passive voice. Likely, our students will find themselves listening to a news report at some point in their lives, so news shows make a good focal point for this activity. Since news outlets are generally obliged to report on events without bias, they often resort to the use of the passive voice.[33] Students have found that imitating a news outlets' use of passive voice can have amusing results. In this project, students can either dodge blame using passive voice, or they can create a news program filled with passive voice reports.

We give them some choice on the topics, which may include the following:

- Politicians lying
- Teachers not grading tests
- Kids forgetting their homework
- Money spent on frivolous items
- Inappropriate clothing worn to school

Allow students to choose any topic that is engaging to them and that they think could make a good podcast script. Working in groups for this activity, we ask students to narrow down their topic, then write a script that relies on the use of passive voice. Students can report on several items, or they can do a more in-depth story on just one. We also allow students to do mock interviews in which the interviewee uses passive voice to avoid blame. A typical script for a single news story might be as follows:

> An important research paper for English class was left at home today. This paper was left on the kitchen counter next to a brown paper bag containing a peanut butter and jelly sandwich. Although this paper was due in English class

---

33. We highly recommend bringing in examples of passive voice in news reporting. You can find news stories from a variety of sources from www.allsides.com.

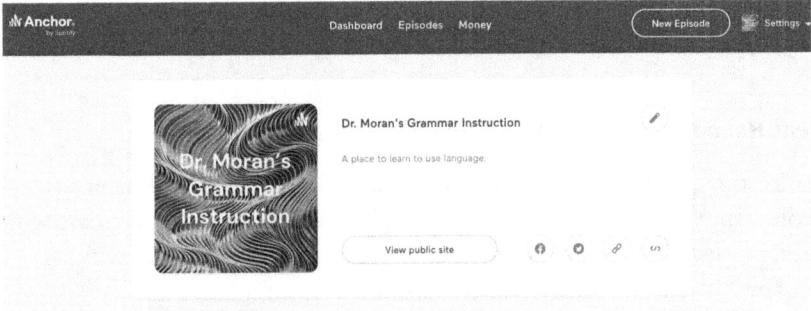

Figure 3.13 Screenshot of Podcasting Dashboard

today, it will not be turned in until tomorrow. The writer of the paper was seen hiding in the bathroom and could not be reached for comment.

Our favorite podcasting tool is Anchor. This digital tool is owned by Spotify and makes the creation and publication of a podcast easy. Anchor allows recordings up to 30 minutes long, so it is perfect for a longer news report. It also links users to Spotify so that they can add music to their podcast. Another tool we love is FlipGrid, which allows for a shorter news report. FlipGrid also records a video of the student; however, if students do not want their pictures to appear, they can choose an emoji to go over their face. Other podcasting tools include Audacity and Soundtrap. Figure 3.13 shows a screenshot from Anchor.

Whatever digital recording tool you decide to use, the point is to encourage students to use the passive voice purposefully to avoid blame.

Why Teach This?

Understanding the uses of passive voice in mainstream media can be an effective reminder to students that news reports—and social media information—are not neutral. The passive voice is a hedging voice; it allows the user to dodge blame, and it avoids taking responsibility for things that have gone wrong. When students recognize this rhetorical effect, they become critical consumers of the news, both on traditional news sites and those that pose as news sites. Additionally, it helps them identify the hedging and dodging from authorities and others that they will inevitably hear throughout their lifetime. In one recent example, the initial police report on George Floyd (who was murdered by officer Derek Chauvin), said that "a suspect" "was ordered to step from his car." The report goes on to say, "At no time were weapons of any type used by anyone involved in this incident."[34] In this case, a public relations director expertly used the passive voice to keep the blame off the officers involved. We want our students to be able to sniff out this

---

34. See https://www.cnn.com/2021/04/21/us/minneapolis-police-george-floyd-death/index.html. For a more complete discussion of this report, and how to bring it into the classroom with language study, see Chapter 5.

tactic—encouraging them to create their own newscasts using passive voice will help in this endeavor.

> **Student Handout: Passive Voice Through Podcasting**
>
> 1. Since this activity involves making a news report, you will need to decide if you want to record an interview, a single story, or a whole newscast with several stories. In your group, decide on the form your podcast will take. Then, discuss the story/interview/stories you will cover.
> 2. Write out the script for the report. You should aim for between one and three minutes long. Your script should include appropriate uses of passive voice. Remember that your use of passive voice should be about avoiding blame.
> 3. Practice reading the script out loud once or twice.
> 4. Open the podcasting digital tool on your internet-enable device. Following the prompts in the tool, record the script for the podcast. Save the recording.
> 5. Provide the URL or podcast information so others can listen.
> 6. Explain to the class how you used the passive voice purposefully to avoid blame.

COLONS AND SEMICOLONS THROUGH TWITTER

Colons and semicolons allow writers to convey nuance, relationships, and connections. They provide numerous sentence possibilities—causal and consequential, persuasive and poetic—with the meanings they suggest. Mastery of these marks often indicates a writer with a confident grasp of language.

While many students are unfamiliar with colon and semicolon conventions in standardized English spaces, and thus reluctant to use them as punctuation, these punctuation marks do show up pretty frequently in digital communication: as elements of common emoticons. We're all familiar with the colon when it's employed as the eyes in the smile emoticon :-), a symbol which itself can be seen as similar in function to that of an actual colon in a sentence.

Stay with us here. When do we use a smile emoticon? When we want to be sure that our previous comment comes across with the positive, lighthearted, or friendly tone that we intend. The emoticon provides some essential information that clarifies the tone of the words that came before. Consider the difference:

- We need to talk about the plan for the weekend.
- We need to talk about the plan for the weekend :-)

The second sentence conveys an emotional nuance (positive, anticipatory, friendly) that is entirely absent from the first, which is at best emotionally neutral. Colons, when used as regular sentence punctuation, do something similar: they offer more specific information about a preceding statement. The form of that information can vary, but it always elaborates on what came before.

A semicolon, meanwhile, appears in the wink emoticon; -). As we know, this symbol communicates an I'm-just-joking sense about the previous statement. For the sake of comparison, here's an example:

- I'm really mad at you.
- I'm really mad at you ;-)

We know which message we'd rather get.

Can we make a similar connection to a semicolon's function as punctuation? Maybe so. While a winking emoticon links a statement to playful intent, a semicolon links two independent clauses that have some close-meaning connection.

> **QUICK REFRESHER: COLONS AND SEMICOLONS**
>
> **Colon:** a punctuation mark that notes that something—a list, a definition, or more information—is about to be provided. A colon usually follows an independent clause:
> - Example: *I plan to take only two things camping this weekend: a tent and my hiking shoes.* In this sentence, the items after the colon (the tent and hiking shoes) clarify what *things* you are taking camping. If the sentence read simply, "I plan to take my tent and hiking shoes camping this weekend," it would not have the same rhetorical effect. The colon provides the extra oomph as if to say, "Hey! Look at this!" Sometimes when a colon is used as a definition marker, it does not follow an independent clause, and the statement sometimes lacks a verb. (Example: *Pizza: the greatest food in the world.*)
>
> **Semicolon:** a punctuation mark that links two independent clauses. The semicolon can be used in place of (1) a comma and conjunction or (2) a period. Typically, a semicolon is used when the two sentences inform one another in some way.
> - Example: *The concert was unbelievably fun; we danced and sang until 1 a.m.* In this sentence, the two independent clauses ("The concert was unbelievably fun" and "We danced and sang until 1 a.m.") are joined together to provide a cohesive, connected idea. The writer could have used a comma and conjunction ("The concert was unbelievably fun, and we danced and sang until 1 a.m."), but it doesn't have the same rhythm and meaning connection. If it helps, the semicolon provides the winking link (think emoticons) that underscores the fact that the concert was fun.

Twitter is a great forum for practicing punctuation because it requires brevity. Tweeters[35] must compress their thoughts into a maximum of 280 characters; diction and punctuation choices take on more importance with this constraint. Students must carefully edit

---

35. Not "twits."

> Mortal Kombat is the epitome of a great video game; it has literally everything. After hours of listening to teachers talk, I only want to do one thing: fight like Scorpion.
> #MortalKombat #gamergirl

Figure 3.14 A tweet Using a Semicolon and Colon

their ideas into a punchy essence, and as tools, the colon and semicolon can help writers pare their language, avoid superfluous words, and make direct connections. Figure 3.14 shows a student tweet that uses both a semicolon and colon.

Once students are comfortable with the functional use of these punctuation marks, we might encourage them to take them up as rhetorical devices. Because semicolons indicate a connection between independent clauses, they can be used to hint at subtle meanings. Consider the examples below:

- Arlo is planning to try out for the varsity basketball team; in other news, he's also president of the Optimist Club.
- Summers in the South always seemed romantic—sweet tea, lemonade, and strolls along the water; when we moved there in August, I soon learned the difference between illusion and reality.

There's something interesting going on with these sentences: the semicolon helps suggest deeper meanings than what we see on the surface. We might detect a bit of snark regarding Arlo's basketball dreams; in the second sentence, there's an interesting tension suggested about depictions of Southern summers versus actual experience. In both cases, the semicolon helps suggest that there's more to the story. Used on a social media platform such as Twitter, such messages hint at deeper meanings.

What about colons? How can students use them in rhetorically deft ways? The power of the colon lies in the ability to bring a statement to an abrupt stop and focus the attention of a reader on what follows.[36] The constraints of social media messaging fit nicely with this function, as we have precious little time to hold a scrolling reader's attention in a digital space. In leveraging the rhetorical techniques of modern propaganda (Hobbs, 2020), colons are a useful way to summarize complex issues in an emphatic, mic-drop fashion:

- When the facts are all on the table, there's no doubt about the greatest gymnast in history: Simone Biles.
- The debate over safety issues evaporated when I rode in my friend's car and realized one overriding fact: convertibles are super fun.

We can help students level-up their rhetorical colon use by helping them identify their passions and positions on various subjects and then work these stances into powerful

---

36. A student once compared the colon's shape to the two barrels of a shotgun: it's a rather startling image, and one that certainly brought us to a halt, just as a colon does in a sentence.

colon-centered statements. Of course, part of our discussion should include the affordances and constraints of this tool (Jones & Hafner, 2021). There's a trade-off to the muscularity of a concluding colon-inflected point, as such statements can serve to shut the door on further discussion. As with all rhetorical options, students must weigh the context of their communication for the advantages and drawbacks of this choice.

Why Teach This?

While semicolons and colons can indicate a level of refinement in student prose, they are more than just decorations or signals of sophistication. Students who understand the rhetorical effect of these punctuation marks can use them to articulate relationships and amplify ideas. A semicolon hints at a more complex connection between sentence elements while a colon serves to emphasize particular items.

Using Twitter to practice applied use of semicolons and colons—or really any other punctuation mark—can help students hone sentences for a specific rhetorical purpose. A tweet stands alone as a testament to a student's understanding of a concept. Although the directions for this activity focus on semicolons and colons, Twitter works as a potential platform for practicing a variety of grammatical concepts.

Student Handout: Semicolons and Colons Through Twitter

1. On your mobile device, download the free Twitter app.
2. Access the class Twitter account.
3. Think of several topics about which you are knowledgeable and feel strongly.
4. Create a tweet in which you suggest a relationship or connection between two ideas with the use of a semicolon. Remember that a semicolon joins two sentences.
5. Create another tweet in which you use a colon to emphasize an idea, truth, or opinion. Remember that what comes before a colon can usually stand as a sentence.
6. Tag your teacher and add any relevant hashtags based on your topic before tweeting.

HYPHENATED ADJECTIVES AND NOUNS THROUGH DIGITAL SCRAPBOOKS

We live in a hyphenated world these days, and we think that's a good thing. Hyphens join concepts to create something new while at the same time preserving the uniqueness of the original elements. A "blue-green ocean" isn't blue or green, but a color in between (or composed of both).[37] And when we consider personal identity, hyphenated concepts hold a lot of potential for helping students express the many facets of who they are.

Though a bit of a cliché, conventional high school stereotypes can serve as a platform for experimenting with hyphens. Jocks, nerds, band geeks, brains, goths, burnouts—the categories may be different in each school, but the concept is the same. Stereotypes

---

37. Sure, teal or turquoise might do the trick as well, but there's something unique in how a hyphenated term maintains the original elements within a new collective. For instance, maybe a blue-green ocean appears blue at certain times and green at others.

reduce the complexity of individuals to a single simple definition. Hyphens, meanwhile, can lead us back to the quirky uniqueness that makes each of us different:

- I'm a part-movie-buff, part-exercise-freak, all-vegetarian kind of person.
- Chang argues that he's radical-centrist-humanist in outlook, while Jo is more left-leaning-pragmatic in her views.
- She loves Rodrick's never-give-up attitude.
- My buddy Regan is a tattooed-normcore-meets-modern-punk-hipster character.
- I met his cousin Nia, who considers herself a semi-motorhead-gamer-full-time chef-and-rapper.

If we're getting technical, we can note that the first three examples above feature hyphenated adjective forms, while the last two are hyphenated nouns. With students, however, we tend to focus much more on what grammar concepts allow us to *do* rather than what they're called by the experts.

While creative hyphen use is all over the place on social media, we can also turn to classics to find examples as well: one of the best mentor texts that uses hyphenated adjectives is Homer's *The Iliad*. In this epic poem, readers can find Homeric "epithets," or descriptive phrases that help paint a picture of a place or person. Since *The Iliad* was sung or spoken, it was important for listeners to remember the vast cast of characters. So, Homer included descriptors like "great-hearted Patroclus," "red-haired Menelaus," and "white-armed Hera." Likewise, places took on cinematic qualities with images like the "wine-dark sea."[38]

Shakespeare also employed hyphenated adjectives and nouns for evocative description of characters. In *Macbeth*, he writes of a "heat-oppressed brain" and "pale-hearted fear," and Macbeth himself calls a servant "whey-face," presumably because his complexion resembles weak, yellow milk (unlikely to be a compliment, we'd guess). The hyphens in these phrases serve to connect the adjectives or nouns to each other to create new concepts. A longer phrase would also do the job (e.g., "a brain oppressed by fear" instead of "heat-oppressed brain" or "fear that turns one's heart pale" instead of "pale-hearted fear") but the rhetorical effect of hyphenation is stronger and more rhythmic. Calling out a villain as a "lily-livered scoundrel" is certainly more colorful than going with the more pedestrian "cowardly scoundrel."

QUICK REFRESHER: HYPHENATED ADJECTIVES AND NOUNS[39]

Hyphenated adjectives: Two or more words connected together with a hyphen that modify a noun:
- The *two-faced*, lying cheater I used to date is now seeing my best friend.

Hyphenated nouns: Two or more words connected together with a hyphen that function as a noun.
- Although he will occasionally eat cucumbers, my dog is definitely a *meat-eater*.

---

38. Presumably red rather than white wine. :)

39. While we provide the definitions here, we would like to emphasize that the goal isn't for students to be able to identify whether they constructed a hyphenated adjective or a hyphenated noun. The goal is to use hyphenation with rhetorical purpose, as the examples above demonstrate.

To help students understand the creative power of hyphenated adjectives and nouns, consider a digital scrapbook: a collage of images and text that provides a visual rendition of a place, person, thing, or feeling. Digital scrapbooks are easy to manipulate and can provide a visceral representation of how hyphenated adjectives and nouns create new concepts with words (Noden, 2011).

Canva is a great option for this work, though there are many other digital scrapbook possibilities out there, including Crello, DesignBold, and Adobe Spark. Students might begin with straightforward depictions of hyphenated concepts (see Figure 3.15) before experimenting in more personal directions with the platform. For instance, digital scrapbooks can serve as visual counternarratives that speak back to stereotypes or generalities about a student's identity, revealing the complexity, hybridity, and nuance in one's identity.

Why Teach This?

Hyphenated adjectives and nouns literally involve the creation of new concepts. Combining and transforming normally separate ideas or elements are key facets of remix and creativity. And while helping students experiment with merging words purposefully will likely lead to more colorful and descriptive writing, perhaps more importantly, such work reinforces the notion of identity as an evolving and complex phenomenon.

That said, a word of caution. Newly minted hyphenated concepts are fairly uncommon in many academic and professional writing forms; "use sparingly" is good advice in these situations. One or two salted in one's writing is usually more than enough. Use too many at once, and we lose their impact and risk coming across as silly or pretentious.

Figure 3.15 Digital Scrapbook Page With Images and Hyphenated Adjectives

Digital scrapbooks help keep overuse to a minimum. Students can use images as a second text to illustrate their hybridized ideas, and the scrapbooks themselves can even be used to fashion a collage of image and text, in effect hyphenating images as well.

Student Handout: Hyphenated Adjectives Through Digital Scrapbooks

1. In your journal, list some of the stereotypes others might assume about you.
2. Next, note four to five details about yourself that reveal the inaccuracy of these stereotypes. How is your identity more complex than a generality?
3. In your writing, try to use at least two hyphenated adjectives or nouns. An example: "I'm a soccer-playing, karaoke-singing, trivia-and-taekwondo master."
4. Using an internet-enabled device, open the digital scrapbook program your teacher recommends and create an account. We recommend *canva.com/education*.
5. Choose one of the collage templates in the program.
6. Create a collage that describes the sentences you wrote in your journal. Use text boxes to include all or part of the sentences as part of your design.
7. Save your work as a .png file on your computer. Share with others!

COMMAS THROUGH TIKTOK

The comma has arguably caused more stress to English teachers and their students than any other grammatical concept. This trouble goes back as far as punctuated language, to the Greeks and Aristophanes (a librarian at Alexandria) who proposed in 3rd century BCE that written language be broken up with a series of dots. Prior to Aristophanes' idea, written text was one endless diatribe with nothing to indicate where ideas began and ended. Aristophanes' dots eventually were modified by Christian monks, and in the 7th century, Isadore of Seville proposed categorizing Aristophanes' system into high, medium, and low dots to indicate the length of pause when reading a sentence. In Isadore's written language, the high dot was supposed to indicate a long pause (*distinctio finalis*), which morphed into our modern-day period. The medium dot (*punctus versus*) indicated a medium pause and morphed into our modern-day semicolon, and the low dot (*subdistinctio*) indicated a brief pause and morphed into the modern-day comma.

From here, language purists, beginning in the 18th century, began to obsess over the "correct" use of the comma. One of the first articles in the *English Journal* in 1917 was titled "Three Rules for the Comma" and reminded readers that "all commas represent pauses, real or imagined" (Routh, 1917, p. 35). This, no doubt, gave rise to the simplistic saying we learned in elementary school: "put a comma when you pause for a breath." The trouble is that each of us breathes in different places, so basically all you're doing is showing people your breathing patterns—not really helpful. Despite all of this, the comma remains one of the most frequently corrected punctuation marks on students' formal papers even once they graduate high school and move on to college (Lunsford & Lunsford, 2008). The rules, whatever they are, never quite sink in.

Although we find language and punctuation fascinating, we don't believe that teachers should spend their valuable time marking up student work for misplaced commas since they rarely lead to misunderstandings.[40] Beyond this, comma correction can be associated with status marking—a phenomenon described by Hairston (1981) in which certain errors associate a writer with a lower socioeconomic class. If we want to empower our students, then we need to avoid peppering their written work with ineffective marks and comments about their comma use. It is, after all, the content that is the most important.

Commas are also slippery grammatical concepts. There are more than 15 different comma functions (Crovitz & Devereaux, 2017), and in some cases, the use of a comma is a rhetorical choice.[41] However, folks who love standardized language[42] tend to love standardized punctuation use, so it is probably reasonable to teach some rules of commas to your students. But like all grammar instruction, you shouldn't say, "Okay, folks! Today we are going to learn about commas! Yay!" Rather, comma instruction should be embedded in the concept that dictates its use. For example, when teaching dependent clauses, it makes sense to teach the rules specific to commas and dependent clauses.

Here, however, we want to give you an example of what comma instruction might look like in digital spaces, so we turn to two concepts, the comma splice and the introductory dependent clause. Let's deal with the splice first.

QUICK REFRESHER: COMMA SPLICES

By Standardized English definitions, comma splices combine two complete sentences (i.e., independent clauses) with nothing more than a comma. The problem here, at least according to convention, is that sentences need a "stronger" rhetorical tool to hold them together. Comma splices can be fixed, typically, by adding an appropriate coordinating conjunction (e.g., and, but, or, etc.) after the comma, or by simply exchanging the comma for a semicolon or period:

- *Example of a comma splice:* Jardin wanted to play football, he quickly decided it wasn't for him.
- *A comma splice changed to Standardized English with a coordinating conjunction:* Jardin wanted to play football, but he quickly decided it wasn't for him.
- *A comma splice changed to Standardized English with a semicolon:* Jardin wanted to play football; he quickly decided it wasn't for him.
- *A comma splice changed to Standardized English with a period:* Jardin wanted to play football. He quickly decided it wasn't for him.

---

40. Yes, we can hear you now: but what about all of those egregious examples of commas gone wrong? *Let's eat grandma* versus *Let's eat, grandma*. Or the viral video of the student reminding everyone of the importance of the Oxford comma (*...my parents, Batman and Superman* versus *... my parents, Batman, and Superman*). Those are lovely little examples of outliers, and people like to lean on them. But in 99% of cases, comma misuse doesn't result in some catastrophic misunderstanding (OMG, he's advocating cannibalism...and of a family member!!!) nor does it really cause an existential crisis about the real identity of one's parents.

41. *Commas can sometimes be problematic punctuation marks.* versus *Commas can, sometimes, be problematic punctuation marks.* Both of these sentences are correct by the rules of Standardized English; however, the rhetorical impact is different. Ain't commas fun?

42. We purposefully use the word "standardized" here instead of "standard" because "standardized" clarifies the idea that the rules and expectations of the English language are constructed by outside forces, which "standardized" denotes, as opposed to the idea that these rules and expectations are innate and absolute, which "standard" implies (Metz, 2019).

Splices aren't high on our list of comma drama. To be blunt, the "rule" for how commas can join independent clauses is completely arbitrary. There's no good reason a comma can't do this work alone except that convention bars it. At the same time, because research suggests that the splice is an error that the public readily identifies as a "status-marking" problem, it's a concern that teachers need to consider. Of course, context matters. Comma splices can be viewed as frustratingly persistent errors (in formal student writing) or rhetorically savvy moves (in online marketing). Just repeating the definition and possible solutions to students isn't likely to be sufficient for deep understanding. But maybe there's a way to discuss how distinct sentence-centric ideas might be joined through the affordances of digital media.

Remix is central to TikTok as a platform, which makes it a rich model of the way ideas are joined grammatically.[43] TikTok's "stitch" affordance literally invites users to build on or respond to an existing text; as TikTok itself puts it, "Stitch is a way to reinterpret and add to another user's content, building on their stories." Sometimes this spliced-in video reaction is a direct response to an explicit invitation from a TikToker, as in the "Tell Me Without Telling Me" challenge. Other stitches aim for humor or irony through incongruity and contrast; in many cases, users have made their content available to be "stitched" into someone else's video, but there's no telling what that next person's response will be.

Basically, a stitch is the video equivalent of uniting two independent clauses in a direct and abrupt way. As with a comma splice, a stitch contains no explicit conjunction; the length constraints of TikTok videos makes such gestures extraneous (and pointless) anyway. The relationship between the two texts is clear through context. We all know this intuitively, because in modern culture, we've been exposed to thousands of video texts that have been composed this way, and we've absorbed their implicit grammar. Jump cuts in film typically aren't confusing, and they're used in various ways (point-counterpoint, statement-reaction, question-response, statement-example) for a whole bunch of purposes.

Why Teach This?

So, how can TikTok stitches and similar remixed digital texts help students understand the comma in this particular function? A possible solution is focusing on context and legitimacy. Video texts such as those on TikTok and similar platforms come with specific conventions. We expect short, quick cuts between scenes or moments. For the most part, we don't need explicit conjunctive tools because we process visual information much differently than we do print information.[44] Noticing these conventions in TikTok stitches can help students understand that splicing is conventionally appropriate in certain contexts. The same is generally true when it comes to texting, in which

---

43. Remember, grammar is ultimately more about communication and shared meaning than automatic rule-following.
44. Of course, conjunctive tools can sometimes be used to connect visual texts for the purposes of humorous or sarcastic commentary (e.g., the "Meanwhile" and "Three Hours Later" memes, which interject these phrases between texts to amplify an effect).

the connection (and intention) between independent ideas is often implied. Consider these two versions of messages:

- It's late, and I'm getting hungry. Can we leave soon?
- it's late, i'm getting hungry, can we leave soon

The first example is in Standardized English, which includes features unnecessary in textspeak. When we text, we typically forego the formalities of written English for the sake of expediency and a focus on immediate meanings above other considerations. The multiple splices in the second example *work* in this context.[45] Helping students notice and think through how texts in multiple modes use conjunctive features (or don't) helps illuminate the conventions of Standardized Written English as simply a matter of context.[46]

Let's try out another common comma issue: the need for this particular punctuation mark following an introductory dependent clause (or really, almost any opening modifier in a sentence). Again, we have a potential status-marking concern[47] that probably warrants attention in the classroom somehow. Noguchi's (1991) simple sentence manipulation techniques are an accessible way for students to eventually gain a sense of sentence modifiers, their movable nature within a sentence, and their attendant comma conventions. We can again turn to digital texts as a way to extend student understanding in applied and analogous ways.

The discussion of memes and their use of dependent and implied independent clauses earlier in this chapter invites discussion about how these texts might be rendered in print. If we consider an opening sentence modifier as a kind of "set up" for a subsequent independent clause (in the same manner as jokes often involve a set-up and a punchline), we can see a comma as playing an important dramatic role. In fact, any kind of text that serves in an anticipatory role for a more complete future text (such as a film teaser trailer or a cliffhanger episode) can help with this understanding. We never go *directly* from a teaser to the movie itself, or *immediately* from a final cliffhanger episode to the next season of a TV show[48]—there's always a dramatic pause in order to generate interest. The same might be said for the comma that demarcates an opening modifier from the rest of the sentence.

Finally, we want to emphasize the possibilities of creative metaphors combined with phone-based video apps as learning tools. It's ridiculously easy to make short films these days. As students work through grammar concepts, considering how they're used for real purposes, they'll inevitably develop their own practical understandings, if not epiphanies. These moments can be the basis for new generative texts, as students use

---

45. Arguably, we could even leave the commas out entirely, though the resulting fused sentence ("it's late i'm getting hungry can we leave soon") might slow down meaning slightly in that the borders of each separate idea aren't immediately clear.
46. In effect, we ask you to consider here a *multimodal code switching of mechanics* as a potentially useful way for students to gain perspective on the comma splice and its fit.
47. "Comma missing from introductory dependent clause" is listed in Hairston's (1981) survey of status-marking errors.
48. Except for when we're binge-watching multiple seasons, of course.

video-type apps like TikTok or YouCut to create rich multimodal explanations that might help others. Keep in mind, just repeating a textbook rule in a new mode is unlikely to be useful. But a fresh metaphor or mnemonic, a new angle or application for thinking about a concept and how it works? That just might be the moment when grammar suddenly shifts from mystery to making sense.[49]

> **Student Handout: Comma Splices Through TikTok**
>
> 1. Working with a partner, sift through TikTok to choose a couple of different videos that you might splice or "Stitch" together. Consider the implications of splicing these videos and how they might amplify or alter the original message(s).
> 2. In the first video that you want to Stitch, click on the "send to" button. Then hit "Stitch."
> 3. Choose up to five seconds of the video.
> 4. Repeat the process with more videos so that you gradually add to the Stitched clip.
> 5. Once you have an original video (created with a compilation of other videos), try creating a comma-spliced sentence or two that mimics the video and the spliced sequence. (Example: The dog knocked the plant over, the baby screamed, the mom took a nap.)
> 6. Defend your choices and tell the class why the splice "works" even though it might be grammatically "incorrect."

A FINAL THOUGHT

Much in the same way we advocate for rhetorical grammar instruction embedded in explorations of how language is used in context, we also advocate for language study to drive your instruction, not the technological tools we discuss in this chapter. Technology is just one of many vehicles to get you to your destination. If one of the digital tools we mentioned does not work for you, don't use it! We are not here to sell technology for your classroom. Rather, we want you to use digital tools to engage students *when appropriate*. At the end of the day, *you* are the best teacher of language study for your students.

REFERENCES

ABC News [@ABC]. (2016, Sept. 26). "Clinton invited several people to the debate, including Mark Cuban, a 9/11 survivor and a domestic abuse survivor." [Tweet]. Twitter. https://twitter.com/ABC/status/780423912232513536

Crovitz, D., & Devereaux, M. (2017). *Grammar to get things done: A practical guide for teachers anchored in real-world usage*. Routledge/NCTE. https://doi.org/10.4324/9781315544410

Crovitz, D., & Devereaux, M. (2019). More grammar to get things done. Routledge.

Crovitz, D., & Moran, C. M. (2020). Analyzing disruptive memes in an age of international interference. *English Journal, 109*(4), 62–69.

Curzan, A., & Adams, M. (2012). How English works: A linguistic introduction (3rd ed.). Pearson.

Devereaux, M.D., & Crovitz, D. (2018). Power play: From grammar to language study. *English Journal, 107,* 19.

Ferdig, R. E., Rasinsinski, T. V., & Pytash, K. (2014). *Using technology to enhance writing*. Solution Tree Press.

---

49. Darren's TikTok example of how he conceives of commas, dependent clauses, and other modifiers at the beginning of a sentence is available at this link: https://vm.tiktok.com/ZMRqkFEGW/

Gee, J. P. (2017). A personal retrospective on the New London Group and its formation. In F. Serafini & E. Gee (Eds.), *Remixing multiliteracies* (pp. 19–34). Teachers College Press.

Hairston, M. (1981). Not all errors are created equal: Nonacademic readers in the professions respond to lapses in usage. *College English, 43*(8), 794-806.

Hicks, T. (2013). *Crafting digital writing: Composing texts across media and genres*. Heinemann.

Hillocks, G. (1986). Research on written composition: New directions for teaching. National Council of Teachers of English.

Hobbs, R. (2020). Mind over media: Propaganda education for a digital age. Norton.

Hyler, J., & Hicks, T. (2017). *From texting to teaching: Grammar instruction in a digital age*. Heinemann.

Jones, R. H., & Hafner, C. A. (2021). *Understanding digital literacies: A practical introduction* (2nd ed.). Routledge. https://doi.org/10.4324/9780203095317

Ito, M., Baumer, S., Bittanti, M., Boyd, D., Cody, R., Herr-Stephenson, R., & Horst, H. A., Lange, P. G., Mahendran, D., Martinez, K. Z., Pascoe, C. J., Perkel, D., Robinson, L., Sims, C., & Tripp, L. et al. (2009). *Hanging out, messing around, and geeking out: Kids living and learning with new media* (1st ed.). The MIT Press.

Krakauer, J. (1997). *Into thin air: A personal account of the Mt. Everest disaster*. Anchor.

Lee, H. (2002/1961). *To kill a mockingbird*. Harper Perennial.

Lunsford, A. A., & Lunsford, K. J. (2008). "Mistakes are a fact of life": A national comparative study. *College Composition and Communication, 59*(4), 781–806.

Metz, M. (2019). Principles to navigate the challenges of teaching English language variation: A guide for nonlinguists. In M. D. Devereaux & C. C. Palmer (Eds.), *Teaching language variation in the classroom: Strategies and models from teachers and linguists* (pp. 69–75). Routledge.

Moran, C. M. (2021). How am I supposed to teach this?: Using Google Cardboards to enhance English language arts learning. In C. M. Moran & M. F. Rice (Eds.), *Virtual and augmented reality in English language arts education*. Rowman & Littlefield/Lexington.

Moran, C. M., & Woodall, M. (2019). 'It was like I was there': Inspiring engagement through virtual reality. *English Journal, 109*(1), 90–96.

National Council of Teachers of English. (2018). Beliefs for integrating technology into the English language arts classroom. https://ncte.org/statement/beliefs-technology-preparation-english-teachers/

Noden, H. (2011). *Image grammar: Teaching grammar as part of the writing process* (2nd ed.). Heinemann.

Noguchi, R. (1991). *Grammar and the teaching of writing: Limits and possibilities*. NCTE.

Palincsar, A. S., & Brown, A. L. (1984). Reciprocal teaching of comprehension-fostering and comprehension-monitoring activities. *Comprehension and Instruction, 1*(2), 117–175.

Pew Research Center. (2019, July 23). *Digital news fact sheet*. https://www.journalism.org/fact-sheet/digital-news/

Routh, J. (1917). Three rules for the comma. *The English Journal, 6*(1), 34–39.

Watson, E. [@emmawatson]. (2018, March 18). "Fake tattoo proofreading position available. Experience with apostrophes a must." [Tweet]. Twitter. https://twitter.com/EmmaWatson/status/970803023856439297

SECTION II

Language Moves in Digital Spaces

CHAPTER 4

Play or Be Played

In this chapter, we'll consider our current digital landscape. How do we interact with technology? How does technology function in our day-to-day lives? Once we explore how our digital worlds act and interact with one another, the next chapter considers how to help students become critical consumers and producers within these contexts.

WHAT DOES IT MEAN TO "PLAY"?

In today's digital environments, it's play or be played.

When we hear the word "play," games probably spring to mind. And most definitely, gaming, gamification, and game-based entertainment have a huge cultural influence in digital spaces. But our notion of play here goes beyond leisure and borrows from Csickszentmihalyi's (2008) idea of "optimal experience" as a central, and even necessary, facet of learning and meaningful life activities (pp. 3–4). Play, in this sense, is engagement with a specific activity where participants enter a state of flow—in this state of flow, specific problems are solved through experience, creativity, and persistence, all with a surrounding sense of meaningful accomplishment. Sounds lovely, right?

Video gaming, athletic competition, and music making are typical examples of experiencing "flow" through play, but the concept extends to any activity where people are engrossed in activities (individually and collaboratively) that they find challenging and rewarding. Think of your own hobbies and affinities; chances are there's an associated experience of play and flow that you know well. It's what brings us back to the things we love doing.

"Play" might thus be shorthand for *authentic and engrossing engagement*. And while creative engagement is possible in many physical-world contexts, it's become a core feature of digital tools and environments. For example, just a few years ago, graphic digital design (and the potential for easy distribution) was only for professionals and experts.[1] Today, however, sites like Canva make sure that your lack of experience is no longer a barrier to creation. Drag-and-drop features, easily adjustable templates, and just-in-time assistance create the "open sandbox" concept of playful and safe experimentation—and this accessibility is now expected when we engage with a digital tool. In digital environments, a company's potential profit is based on providing novices with positive experiences: show

---

1. With its massive array of tools and lack of tutorials for novices, Adobe's Photoshop is a classic example of an application long communicating an "only for pros" sensibility.

people how painless and fun it can be to create and share digital posters and graphics, and maybe they'll find the resource useful enough to upgrade to a paid account. The creators of digital tools understand that "make it fun and easy to use" is a necessity.

There is a unifying thread among all the spaces we've discussed thus far: we can do challenging things and improve because those spaces[2] value experimentation and creativity. Failure is not just normal *but expected* and screwing up is not a terminal moment of stigma but rather a step to learning more and eventually succeeding.[3]

Broadly speaking then, play requires us to *engage without fear of failure* (because failure is necessary for growth). The flip side of this idea, however, is that play also expects that we *engage without fear of perfection*. A space or experience that allows judgment-free risk-taking is only beneficial if we understand learning as applied, partial, incremental, contingent, non-linear, and forever incomplete and ongoing. We also learn some important things about ourselves through play: Are we willing to continue when we encounter difficulties? Are we willing to accept progress over perfection? This type of playful stance toward engagement and this type of self-assessment is often rewarded in many digital spaces, environments, and platforms.

Finally, we can't deny that at the heart of playfulness lives a trickster spirit. Play is routinized in many ways, as in the myriad rules and conduct codes of games and sports. Likewise, playing a song in a band means following patterns and meeting mutual expectations. But as any fan of jazz knows, experimentation and improvisation are often intertwined with conventional structures. Playing by the rules sometimes means that the rules are called into question. Engagement and creativity emerge as a blend of knowledge, boldness, and inspiration—and sometimes mischief and skepticism. This can be troubling ground. Some people *really like* the rules because of the safety and stability they provide. But creative play can be viewed as a kind of "good trouble," spurring us toward new ideas and perspectives that enlarge artistic possibility (Beete, 2021).

WHAT DOES IT MEAN TO "BE PLAYED"?

In contrast to the creative engagement at the center of play, no one wants to *be played*.

As the grammatical structure of the phrase suggests, when we're "played," we become objects, spotlighted for ridicule or pity. We're targeted or manipulated by others, exposed as foolish or gullible, ripped off, turned into victims. We're all familiar with the standard cautions in our digital lives to protect against getting scammed. Some of the more clumsy con-artist efforts—the sketchy links and garbled syntax of get-rich-quick opportunities—now mostly serve as who-could-ever-fall-for-this comedy. But the "being played" concept is way more complex than potentially getting clowned by a foreign prince in need of desperate help with a million-dollar bank transfer.

First off, to take part in the digital ecosystem means that to some degree, we willingly *allow* ourselves to be played in certain contexts. Store loyalty programs are a good

---

2. Such as gaming, sports, music, digital creation…

3. This notion is what makes video games so compelling for many people. Losing (or "dying") is a momentary setback that yields new knowledge: "*that* didn't work, but no worries—the setback is minimal, and I'll try something different."

example where we sacrifice some privacy in return for something of value. We pay less money for the things we want, and in return, the company gets detailed digital data about who we are as customers: when and where we shop, the products we buy, how much we spend, the coupons we use (or don't use), the brands we favor, and so on. Like it or not, we actually agree to this kind of relationship almost every time we open an app or a browser.[4] And while we each can determine whether or not the benefits of a store membership are worth the costs, similar compromises in digital terrain are far less equal or evident (Watts, 2019; Wylie, 2019).

Here's an example. How much does it cost to create a Twitter, Instagram, or TikTok account? The obvious answer—*duh, nothing, they're free*—isn't really accurate. As cultural theorists have pointed out, when we don't pay for a service or product, it often means that *we ourselves are the product*.[5] That is, our willing participation on a platform—our clicks, likes, shares, time on screen, scrolling rate, friends, favorites, comments, visits per day, geotracked movement, and dozens of other markers—amounts to a product that can be collected, analyzed, and sold. Our presence and actions produce *data*, and with the help of complex computer algorithms and machine learning, that data is transformed into detailed and individualized profiles: who we are, what we do, what we like and don't like, what we want, what we believe. This information is immensely valuable to organizations intending to target us with specific messages. We've all probably experienced this phenomenon in its most basic commercial form. Spend some time browsing bird feeders online for grandma's birthday, and suddenly your social media timeline is peppered with advertisements for all manner of hangable seed dispensaries.[6]

What's that? You say you didn't agree to this kind of behavior tracking, let alone consent to others making money from it? Actually, you did when you didn't-read-but-still-agreed-to the "Terms of Service" for the various websites, networking platforms, and mobile apps that you use. *But that material is incomprehensible! No one reads it!* Exactly. The dry, legalistic, impenetrable prose of these documents is an intentional language choice. Internet-based companies aren't particularly interested in making their terms of service easy to understand, as doing so would make more evident the costs involved in using their technology. The battle-scarred consumer veterans among us have a typical response to these facts (*caveat emptor*: let the buyer beware!), but this warning feels somewhat cynical given modern digital realities and human nature. It's always we the customers who must change our habits, not businesses and corporations, who are free to market themselves as friendly hubs of community and connection while monetizing user data for advertising revenue—and, as it turns out, much more (Wylie, 2019). The consumer only has power when other viable options exist. The monopolistic nature of Facebook, Google, and other digital giants means that opting out is effectively a form of self-exile, a difficult prospect for social creatures.

---

4. This relationship is such an inevitable element of modern digital life that we considered calling this chapter "Play and Be Played." The modern internet has been commodified, and it's difficult to avoid playing along.
5. Oremus (2018) puts it this way: "If you aren't paying for it with money, you're paying for it in other ways."
6. Always-listening voice-command devices such as Apple's Siri and Amazon's Alexa similarly implicate tech companies and their data collection in our daily lives.

TO PLAY OR BE PLAYED IN OUR MODERN AGE OF PROPAGANDA

Let's pull back and lower the temperature a bit. It's easy (and sometimes satisfying) to fall into the outrage trap, and it can be tempting to position internet companies as predators, luring us into fun-filled social media spaces while actively hiding the costs. But there's clearly a power differential at work here—and someone's inevitably getting played to some degree.

In her 2020 book *Mind Over Media: Propaganda for a Digital Age*, media literacy scholar Renee Hobbs argues for an intriguing framework for understanding, analyzing, and creating digital texts. Hobbs (2020) makes the point that much of digital communication can best be understood as modern *propaganda*, an understandably loaded term that needs some recovery from conventional classroom use. As traditionally encountered in school, propaganda is a phenomenon anchored in the geopolitics of the past and understandably colored with negative association. Modern digital modes, however, can be viewed as vectors of propaganda—literally, the *propagation* of ideas, perspectives, and information intended to influence the thinking of others.

Any kind of public communication that seeks to persuade—from advertising and organized advocacy to a "slacktivist"[7] sharing a political meme—fits into the category of propaganda. In this sense, propaganda isn't a tactic from our distant history. Rather, it's a foundational dimension of modern texts proliferated through digital channels and spaces. And importantly, propaganda isn't automatically negative; it's a rhetorical tool that can be used for various purposes, many of them legitimate. When we advocate publicly for issues we care about by sharing bite-size content—memes, headlines, and visual material through our social channels—we are *doing propaganda*. Of course, we're unlikely to see it that way, since we typically think our views are correct and thus that we're justified in spreading such information (and meanwhile the negative charge of the word "propaganda" makes it more easily directed at the supposed exaggerations and distortions of those who think differently). Hobbs (2020) calls for a modern propaganda education in which students both critically analyze and *create* modern propagandistic texts across multiple contexts as a means of understanding the power, impact, and relevance of these choices.

INTRODUCING PROPAGANDA TO STUDENTS

If we are going to help students consider digital propaganda and its rhetorical anchors, we need to provide them with some questions:

- What topic or issue is the subject of the text?
- What specific audience is targeted by this text?
- How does the text simplify, exaggerate, or distort complex concepts?
- How does the text minimize, ignore, or mischaracterize what others believe?
- What kind of specific action is the text designed to spur?

Although not a comprehensive checklist (we dislike checklists; see Chapter 2), these questions are useful for exploring issues of power, identity, and choice as they manifest through language and other modes of communication.

---

7. A slacktivist (i.e., "slacker" + "activist") is someone whose social or political activism is limited to social media displays.

Consider what a discussion about propaganda might look like around these texts:

- A digital ad for the right-wing *Washington Times* asking, "Tired of being LECTURED, MOCKED, and LIED to by the mainstream media?"
- A customizable app-based hip hop-branded fast-food bundle (Kelso, 2021)
- A meme stating that illegal immigrants are spreading COVID-19
- A fashion influencer's Instagram feed

Powerful but fairly familiar forces—companies, celebrities, public advocates, politicians—leverage digital language for their own interests. They create and maintain digital presences through propaganda. We can help students specifically study these efforts in order to gain familiarity and fluency with these tactics.

But these loud voices aren't the only players online. A bigger game is afoot, one potentially damaging to the shared assumptions we hold as citizens in a democracy.

DIGITAL DISRUPTION

Most of us use app-based smartphones each day as a normal part of our lives. We're so used to the affordances of these gadgets that it can sometimes be difficult to clearly see the extent to which they've altered how we live and communicate, especially in how we engage with information about the world.

We like to think of the revolution of digital technology in our lives as a *convergence* of several different factors, the ramifications of which are only just becoming clear. Let's take a look at some of these factors, understanding that, ultimately, we're going to land on a vital aspect of English language arts: *the connection between language use and how we understand the world*. In the paragraphs below, we've italicized concepts that are simultaneously converging and, as a result, fundamentally challenging how people understand truth and reality.

Converging Strands

Not long ago, smartphones (characterized by their touchscreen *app-centric interaction*) were a small category of mobile device amidst the clunky flip-phone horde. Now most of us carry these advanced devices, which have integrated many of the functions of earlier technologies. At their most transformative, our phones meld our real-world and digital lives together in an everyday, moment-to-moment fashion. As cell phone technology and usage advances, so does our *ubiquitous connectivity*. Only the most remote areas are now without cell coverage, and wifi is the norm anywhere that people gather: we are almost always available to the internet. Meanwhile, the evolution of *participatory digital culture* means that any of us can be digital content creators as well as consumers. Apps are increasingly designed for ease of participation and engagement, from TikTok's stitch feature to tap-and-drag filmmaking apps such as YouCut. Plentiful user-created tutorials easily on-ramp newcomers. Conventional barriers to mass publication and even fame have been removed.

These changes are simultaneous with the *disruption of legacy media*. To be blunt, the news these days isn't what the news used to be. The previous model of the "news industry"—featuring large media companies and professional editors vetting, curating, and producing news through regional newspapers and nightly TV news programming—has been completely changed by internet technologies. Many Americans now get their news through their social media feeds on platforms unregulated by the Federal Communications Commission, which means that the conventional guardrails of expertise and fact-checking, along with the laws concerning truth in advertising and the penalties for broadcasting false information, do not apply in this realm.[8] Not surprisingly, this means that social media sites have become fertile territory for the proliferation of misinformation, alternate truths, conspiracy theories, and systematic efforts to polarize Americans and inflame social divisions.

So if we're increasingly connected online, and if we're getting our news from unregulated sources, shouldn't we be teaching students how to become savvy online consumers and creators? Shouldn't we discuss how technology works in our lives and theirs?

TECHNOLOGY CAN BE EMANCIPATORY … OR REPRESSIVE

Let's take stock of where we—and our students—stand at this moment. Our phones are the most convenient machines for shared information and creativity in history, with collaborative possibilities for liberatory human potential that are only beginning to unfold. Yet these same technologies can be used for not-so-grand motives, ranging from the mildly distasteful to the socially repressive and destructive. It's not a stretch to say that one end of this symbolic spectrum is represented by Juneteenth and its emancipatory celebration of freedom. The other end finds its avatar in January 6, a date that will forever be associated with the storming of the U.S. Capitol.

The early techno-critic Postman (1993) once noted that with each technological development, we gain some new affordance or ability, but we also lose something as well. We tend to be hyper-aware of the benefits of each new tech advancement. The costs, however, are usually hidden, often purposefully so. We must grapple with both ends of the technological spectrum, and question how technology affects our own understanding of the communities and country in which we live. With the negative dimensions of digital technology and the threats posed to individual freedoms and a democratic society, the study of language in this project is central.

REFERENCES

Beete, P. (2021, February 24). Artists reflect on what it means to make good trouble. Arts.Gov. https://www.arts.gov/stories/blog/2021/artists-reflect-what-it-means-make-good-trouble
Csickszentmihalyi, M. (2008). *Flow: The psychology of optimal performance*. Harper Perennial.
Hobbs, R. (2020). *Mind over media: Propaganda education for a digital age*. Norton.
Kelso, A. (2021, February 2). Taco bell's new $5 customizable box is only available through its digital channels. *Forbes*. https://www.forbes.com/sites/aliciakelso/2021/02/02/taco-bells-new-5-customizable-box-is-only-available-through-its-digital-channels/?sh=57b030b22ce2
Oremus, W. (2018, April 27). *Are you really the product? Slate.com*. https://slate.com/technology/2018/04/are-you-really-facebooks-product-the-history-of-a-Dangerous-idea.html
Postman, N. (1993). *The end of education*. Random House.
Watts, C. (2019). *Messing with the enemy: Surviving in a social media world of hackers, terrorists, Russians, and fake news* (Reprint ed.). Harper Paperbacks.
Wylie, C. (2019). *Mindf*ck: Cambridge Analytica and the plot to break America*. Random House.

---

8. Another effect of this shift: traditional media companies slashing reporting budgets, embracing clickbait tactics, and pay-walling online content in order to compete in the new "attention economy."

CHAPTER 5

Grammar at Work in Digital Texts

There's a world of digital texts and spaces that might be discussed in a classroom; likewise, students will have a diversity of interests, experiences, and skill levels that you'll want to consider. For each of the areas that follow, we offer a range of categories, topics, and frameworks that can help you meet students wherever they might be. But before we get into the *how*, we need to talk about a critical component of digital literacy: creativity, and how it needs to be redefined in classroom spaces.

CREATIVE AND CRITICAL POTENTIAL: DIGITAL LITERACIES FOR A DIGITAL CITIZENRY

"Creativity" is one of those amorphous concepts that often ends up being treated as a genetic predisposition rather than a universal trait. By the time young people hit high school, many have internalized the idea that they're not creative[1] (similar to the way that many of them believe themselves to be naturally "bad writers"). Conventional ideas of creativity invoke individual idiosyncrasy and ideas that seem to emerge from the muse-inspired mists of the mind. It's no use touting digital tools for their creative potential if the pathways and processes of creativity are left to the whimsy and inscrutable genius of only a few.

Fortunately, a way forward exists. Writer and filmmaker Kirby Ferguson (2021) argues that creativity has three basic elements, all of which importantly involve building on what others have previously created: copying, combining, and transforming. These components are all part of the broader concept of *remix*, which Ferguson maintains is the engine that drives all creative work.[2]

Let's note first that these ideas clash with some pretty sacrosanct English language arts dogma, especially that first activity. "Copying" is plagued with bad associations, from old-fashioned punishment[3] all the way up to plagiarism, the granddaddy of academic crimes.

---

1. The siloing of artistic interests as careers only suitable for specific kinds of people no doubt contributes to this idea, as when specific company employees are referred to as the "creatives."
2. All of Ferguson's intriguing videos detailing these concepts are available through his website at https://www.everythingisaremix.info/.
3. As in Bart's chalkboard purgatory in the opening credits of every episode of *The Simpsons*.

And yet. It's a simple truth that copying is the first step in learning just about anything, from our ABCs to dance moves to public speaking. We might have fancier terminology when we're coming at it from a pedagogical perspective—calling it "modeling" or "directed practice" or some other gussied-up term—but imitating the moves of those who are more experienced is how humans materialize, instantiate, and internalize[4] learning. Our "copying is cheating" hang-ups derive from an educational culture of stand-alone testing and atomized assessment. Exit the classroom and head outside to the school soccer field, and you'll see a completely different vision of practice and applied learning. If we want to see legit growth, then copying the experts is a good place to begin.

Ferguson's (2021) other two components, *combining* and *transforming*, have a glancing connection to conventional ELA assignments. When we ask students to incorporate outside sources in their argumentative or research-based essays and to use quotation and paraphrasing in doing so, we're essentially asking them to *combine* texts in the creation of new work. The same is true when students create a poster or collage demonstrating their understanding of a character's worldview. More divergent activities, such as asking students to adapt a scene from *Romeo and Juliet* in a modern context, are typical examples of *transforming* existing work into something new. The fundamentals of creativity are already a part of ELA classrooms, if only tangentially and in limited form.

Digital affordances supercharge the potential of these creative elements through multimodal remix culture. In *Understanding Digital Literacies* (2021), Jones & Hafner begin by listing examples of the ways that technology has transformed creative possibilities, allowing us to do what we couldn't do before. Check out a few of the ways we can be "literate" that simply didn't exist a few years ago:

- Composing: the ability to create complex multimodal documents (such as Instagram "stories") that combine words, graphics, video, and audio.
- Assessing reality in digital spaces: the ability to separate the "true" from the "fake" in a complex information ecosystem.
- Negotiating online spaces: the ability to create and maintain dynamic online profiles and manage large and complex online social networks.
- Curating identity: the ability to manage constant surveillance by peers and private companies and to protect one's personal data and "identity" from being misused by others.

Importantly, spontaneous and completely original material *is not really a thing* in digital spaces.[5] Indeed, as Ferguson (2021) puts it, "everything is a remix." The *expectation* is that people will copy, combine, and transform what others have done, immediately publish this chimera, and then fully expect others to potentially do the same with this new work. Digital tools and spaces function as a massive counterweight to the conventional legal concept of copyright, which has been distorted over the last century to hyper-privilege those with formal claims of ownership (whether

---

4. Speaking of fancy terminology...
5. Nor is it a thing "in real life," once we get beyond the stereotype of the solitary genius scribbling away in a garret.

or not this claim is actually connected to creation of any kind[6]). As Hobbs (2020) points out, the point of copyright protection is not just to provide *temporary and limited* protection for creators but to allow others to use existing works in their own creations, thus spurring cultural growth. The geyser of remixed user-created digital content on sites such as TikTok suggests what's possible when technology overtakes status quo assumptions.

For our purposes, the creative reality of remix has important ramifications for how we talk about grammar, language, and meaning with students. In the next section, we delve into some of the possibilities.

THE HUMOR, LINGO, AND COMMUNITY OF DIGITAL TEXTS AND SPACES

Internet memes can be an engaging place to begin conversations of remix, language, and meaning. Meme culture now saturates popular culture, and your students will no doubt be familiar with such texts. Communicating through digital memes means condensing a message into a short and memorable message, and as we've discussed, just about every meme format or template follows particular rules of usage and convention. Of course, not all meme forms are suitable for the classroom. Search for "clean memes," paying particular attention to how grammatical structures are necessary for communicating humor and irony. We provide more ideas on how to use memes in Chapter 3.

As Hobbs (2020) notes, memes are sometimes the vehicles for persuasive perspectives. If appropriate to your context, students can experiment with expressing their positionality on social, political, and linguistic issues, again acknowledging the usage conventions specific to the meme, such as the examples in Figure 5.1.

The emerging scholarly area of *critical memetic literacy* provides a framework for students to consider the rhetorical context of memes. For instance, the questions below

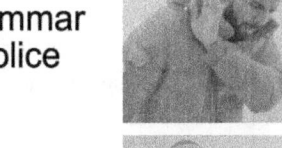

Figure 5.1 Memes Used to Advocate

---

6. The legal holder of a copyright is frequently not the creator of the original work. Michael Jackson once bought the entire back catalog of the Beatles, thus becoming the legal copyright holder.

can help students understand how memes summarize (and inevitably simplify or exaggerate) complex issues:

- Have you seen this meme before? When and where? How was it used?
- Who or what is pictured? Who would recognize these elements?
- What reaction might people have to this meme? Why would they have this reaction?
- Why do you think this picture was selected to accompany this message? What is the effect of this combination?
- Could you still understand the message even if you didn't recognize the elements pictured? Why or why not?
- How do these elements combine to create an overall message?
- What stance does the author take on the topic at hand? (Harvey & Palese, 2018)

Applied, for instance, to the Frodo/clean water meme, these questions can help students gain contextual understanding of how such texts work. We can push forward, however, searching for the boundaries of the message:

- How does the language in the text represent reality?
- What ways might someone resist or object to the stance taken?
- What are the limitations of this form for the message?

These questions tackle the notion of *affordances and constraints* (Jones & Hafner, 2021). In interrogating memes for how they capture and distort ideas and in experimenting with this form themselves, students can gain a deeper understanding of both the potential and the limits of the genre.

Memes, reaction GIFs, and similar texts are now common in our digital communication. When your students are ready, you might ask them to take up the role of *cultural ethnographers*. Multimodal texts don't exist in a vacuum, and the remix capacities of digital technology mean that images are easily unmoored from previous contexts and put to new purposes, often with some controversy.

The phenomenon of "digital blackface" is a case in point. So-called "reaction GIFs" are common app options for digital communication, used to convey a range of emotions: surprise, confusion, disgust, and so on. The prevalence of people of color with exaggerated expressions, however, can echo the racist caricatures of Jim Crow and blackface vaudeville, in which white actors amplified negative stereotypes and imagery. Stereotypes of poor people of color have long been a source of amusement for mainstream White society,[7] and contemporary conversations about cultural appropriation (versus "appreciation") are part of a wider critical questioning of identity, representation, and our obligations to one another.[8] As students gain skill with the power of memetic communication to convey messaging, they can ask critical questions about particular memes, GIFs, and remixed texts.

---

7. Antoine Dodson ("hide yo kids, hide yo wife") and Sweet Brown ("ain't nobody got time for that") are memorable examples: disadvantaged Black folk in distress whose media representations were remixed for laughs without their consent.

8. See Chapter 7 for a deeper discussion of linguistic and cultural appropriation.

Finally, students can explore, analyze, and take up the language of new digital spaces for their own uses. TikTok, for instance, has a multimodal lingo all its own ("for you page," user-created tutorials, graphics conventions, and various hashtags of specialized interest groups such as #FitTok, #booktok, and #cottagecore) indicating familiarity and expertise. A systematic examination of the lingo for a particular trend, affinity group, hashtag, or phenomenon helps students practice the critical distance that in turn can lead to judicious creation in these realms (see Chapter 2 on critical digital literacy and belonging).

THE LANGUAGE TACTICS OF DIGITAL ADVERTISING AND VIRAL MARKETING

English teachers have long used advertisements as an example of persuasive texts, often within the familiar framework of the Aristotelian appeals. Given that advertising surrounds us in a consumer culture, such texts are familiar to students and can be a fruitful way of examining grammar in action. Perhaps the most useful approach with this work is asking students to consider how conventional "incorrect" usage is a common feature in advertising texts.

The prevalence of fragments, creative punctuation, and unorthodox sentence structures is usually considered through the lens of genre-specific license: basically, "the rules are different for advertisers." But in terms of intent and audience, analyzing and practicing these tactics themselves can help students make more sophisticated rhetorical decisions in their own composing. Outside of advertising, when might the following be acceptable as intentional, and why?

- A sentence fragment
- A single word
- A sentence as a single paragraph
- A comma splice

Digital advertising relies on punchy language and imagery given how quickly our attention can wander online. Of course, companies know this, so they've adapted their strategies with each digital evolution. We're familiar with Facebook and YouTube's ubiquitous advertising, but almost any platform is a fresh opportunity for selling and marketing. The popularity of the video-game streaming and networking site Twitch, for example, has companies such as Taco Bell and Honda getting creative with their marketing and promotions. How can these developments be discussed from a grammatical perspective?

One flexible approach is encouraging students to take an *ethnographic stance* toward digital advertising (Brauer & Clark, 2008). Ethnography is the study of specific cultural phenomena (such as SoCal skateboarding lingo or Appalachian shape note singing), often from the perspective of those within that culture. When students think as ethnographers, they inquire about the specific cultural context in which texts are created, distributed, and received. They ask specific questions about intention, textual construction, and audience reception in order to better understand these texts. Putting on a "cultural investigator" hat can create distance from familiar activities and experiences that we might not normally think twice about. Students can create their own "autoethnographies,"[9] complete with hyperlinks and images, to describe their own interactions with advertising or digital spaces.

The social media channels of influencers are also sites of rich language use; savvy celebrities cultivate relationships with fans in these spaces, coming across as personal and authentic rather than corporate and phony. From an ethnographic perspective, students can analyze the feed of a particular musician, star, or performer they follow for how language and image work to create a sense of community. For example, when Meghan Markle (the Duchess of Sussex) was expecting her son Archie, she posted an announcement on Instagram—a non-traditional decision that was seen as "inclusive" and "down-to-earth" rather than stuffy or typically royal. The mega-star Taylor Swift likewise uses her social media feeds to interact directly with her fans in ways that appear authentic and unplanned.

THE STATE AND THE INDIVIDUAL: DIGITAL DEVICES, UBIQUITOUS VIDEO, AND THE NATURE OF REALITY

Digital video has become a common aspect of our modern mediated lives so quickly that we might skip past the enormity of this development. Mobile devices and constant connectivity mean that we all have video cameras in our pockets with an instant audience. Streaming capability makes all of us a potential vector for events as they happen. This technology is both a force for liberation and the spread of factual information—as well as a potential threat to authority. Suddenly, the official version of events can be challenged with immediate and direct video evidence from anyone present at the scene, and even though everyone might *look* at the same video footage, people tend to *see* different things. That is, viewers translate what's on a screen to fit their understanding of the world.

The ubiquity of digital video can reveal episodes of language use intended to obscure, minimize, redefine, or outright shift what is real or true. Video footage can certainly be subject to interpretation. But its sheer power to represent reality provides fascinating opportunities to study language, story, and grammar as reality-shaping tools.

Digital videos and the language surrounding them are ripe for rhetorical discussions. Below we provide three recent examples of how events captured on video can be interpreted across a wide spectrum. Close examination of videos and the rhetoric surrounding them can help our students become savvy digital consumers and critical purveyors of the ideas of truth and justice.

George Floyd

The cellphone video of George Floyd's murder by a Minneapolis police officer is understandably burned into our collective memory. Less well-known is the preliminary police report of this event, which tells a different story:

> Two officers arrived and located the suspect, a male believed to be in his 40s, in his car. He was ordered to step from his car. After he got out, he physically

---

9. An autoethnography is a close study of an aspect of one's own culture.

resisted officers. Officers were able to get the suspect into handcuffs and noted he appeared to be suffering medical distress. Officers called for an ambulance. He was transported to Hennepin County Medical Center by ambulance where he died a short time later. [...] At no time were weapons of any type used by anyone involved in this incident.

(Bump, 2021)

We might ask students to consider this passage for its specific language moves. Questions such as the following—which require further research on the part of students—get at the nexus of language, representation, and reality. We've included some possibilities in italics to get you started:

- What is truthful in this statement, and what is not?
  While all the sentences here might be considered generally accurate, the statement omits vital events between sentences four and five. Arguably, this kind of statement can be seen as misleading, and though each sentence has a basis in fact, together they do not portray an accurate picture of events.
- How has language been used to obscure what happened or imply a different set of facts than the reality?
  The omission of crucial events—namely Officer Derek Chauvin kneeling on Floyd's neck for more than nine minutes—presents a very different picture of reality. The statement also mentions that no weapons were used during the incident in what might be seen as an attempt to distance any specific actions of police with Floyd's death.
- How might some people interpret video differently than others? Are there common facts that can be agreed upon?
  Most definitely people can interpret video differently; a fight caught on film might be seen as an attack by some and self-defense by others. The "meaning" of Chauvin kneeling on Floyd's neck was disputed during Chauvin's subsequent murder trial, with the defense arguing that Chauvin was following established police procedure with his actions. Most people, however—including the jury—saw Chauvin's actions as clearly criminal. He was convicted of all charges, including second- and third-degree murder.

Rand Paul Incident

In 2020, Kentucky senator Rand Paul and his wife encountered a group of protestors outside the Republican National Convention following then-President Trump's speech. Escorted by police, the couple walked for a block or so to their hotel as the crowd followed along shouting slogans at the senator.[10] At one point, a protester pushed an officer, who knocked into Paul.[11]

Later that evening, Paul tweeted about the incident (Figure 5.2):

---

10. Notably, "Say her name!" and "Her name is Breonna Taylor!" in reference to the African American woman killed in her Louisville apartment by police several months earlier.
11. Of course, this description is our version of the scene. Take a look at the video footage—do you think we used language accurately?

Figure 5.2 Rand Paul tweet

The senator characterized the episode as a life-threatening attack by a "crazed mob." In the past, video footage of the event either wouldn't exist or be gate-kept by corporate media, but as we all know, times have changed. Students might view the video[12] of the event and consider the kinds of questions listed below:

- Does Paul's version of events align with the video footage?
- How does Paul's version amplify, marginalize, or silence the voices of particular people?
- What might be a more accurate characterization of the actions of the crowd?
- How might the crowd's actions be characterized to serve different purposes?
- What might be the possible consequences of Paul's claims if video footage didn't exist? (He's a relatively powerful person, after all.)
- Paul was the sponsor of the "Justice for Breonna Taylor Act," which would have prohibited the kind of "no-knock" warrants that led to her death. How does this fact affect interpretations of this event, if at all?
- How might a revised version of Paul's tweet read?

January 6 Insurrection

On January 6, 2021, the U.S. Capitol was surrounded by thousands of Trump supporters attending that day's "Stop the Steal" rally. Protestors destroyed barricades, fought with police, and stormed the Capitol building itself. Hundreds of insurrectionists broke into

---

12. https://youtu.be/Oprrd6c4tX4

the building in an effort to overturn the results of the 2020 presidential election. Much of that day was captured on film, both outside and within the Capitol.

Given that by their own admission, the insurrectionists were acting at the encouragement of President Donald Trump (Barry et al., 2021), it's perhaps not surprising that various Republican representatives later issued public statements seeking to redefine these video scenes.[13] Here are a few examples:

- Rep. Andrew Clyde: "there were some rioters and some who committed acts of vandalism. But let me be clear: there was no insurrection. […] Watching the TV footage of those who entered the Capitol and walked through Statuary Hall showed people in an orderly fashion staying between the stanchions and ropes taking videos and pictures. You know, if you didn't know the TV footage was a video from January the 6th, you would actually think it was a normal tourist visit."
- Rep. Ralph Norman: "I don't know who did a poll to say that [the insurrectionists] were Trump supporters."
- Rep. Paul Gosar: "The truth is being censored and covered up, and as a result, the DOJ is harassing peaceful patriots across the country."
- Sen. Ron Johnson: the insurrectionists were composed of "plainclothes militants, agents provocateurs, fake Trump protesters, and a disciplined, uniform, column of attackers" (Aldridge, 2021).

Politicians are well adept at using words to reach particular ends; it's very unlikely that these comments are happenstance, the product of random or accidental musings. The coordinated effort to downplay these seditious attacks on both the Capitol and the democratic processes begins with attempts to shift understandings of the events *through language*. Teachers seeking to help students understand the intersection of language, power, and truth can use these moments as teaching tools. The questions below can help:

- How do the language moves of politicians simultaneously acknowledge and redefine the reality of the insurrection?
- How is this language used to distract from or cast doubt upon shared understandings?
- What are the implications of the nouns at work in these and similar statements (i.e., patriots, protestors, rioters, mob, insurrectionists, tourists, etc.)?
- What are the implications of each of these nouns in terms of intention and responsibility?

TEXTS DESIGNED FOR DIVISION AND DISCORD: THE LANGUAGE CONVENTIONS OF CONSPIRACY THEORIES AND MISINFORMATION

Most of us try to avoid unnecessary drama in our lives, and part of growing up is figuring out how to use language to solve (rather than exacerbate) problems involving other people. Adolescence is marked by this struggle to take into consideration the feelings,

---

13. These efforts continue at the time of this writing, as efforts to create an independent and bipartisan commission to investigate the insurrection were recently blocked by Senate Republicans.

perspectives, and needs of others, and one marker of adulthood is using language to not just get what you want but to *preserve and strengthen relationships*.

Modern digital affordances, however, have amplified language use for a very different purpose: emphasizing division, hardening stereotypes, and portraying fellow citizens as enemies. While most of us likely find such purposes repugnant, those who seek to separate us—including hostile foreign states and their agents, domestic terrorist groups, anarchists, fraudsters, unethical companies, and anti-democratic interests—are hard at work microtargeting us through our social media channels in order to fuel fear, anger, and distrust (Singer & Brooking, 2019; Watts, 2019; Wylie, 2019). As a digitally savvy teacher, you can help students develop a critical understanding of these tactics through specific grammatical analysis. The syntactical tactics below are typical in texts intended to mislead and inflame through division.

Declaratives and Imperatives

Most of us are familiar with clickbait when we see it, the silly headlines suggesting provocative content ("You Won't Believe What This Videocam Caught…") and supposed listicle[14] insight. Misinformation and conspiracy theories often use the same tactics but also draw upon the conventional trappings of news headlines to masquerade as real. Consider the examples below:

- "State Gives Cops the Green Light To Shoot DAPL Protesters On Sight" (Levin, 2017)
- "Biden's Climate Requirements: Cut 90% of Red Meat from Diet" (Brewster, 2021; Swenson, 2021)

Both of these statements seem legitimate but aren't. They adhere to news headline conventions, with short declarative phrasing that summarizes a piece of information. If you're concerned about police brutality, or if you believe that President Biden's policies are too extreme, encountering these headlines on a social media feed might trigger your predetermined suspicions. Instead of a careful perusal of the facts, many of us might be inclined to act immediately, sharing or liking what we've seen in an effort to publicize an injustice.

With Students…

You can help students understand the contours of headline convention and manipulation with some focused practice:

1. Ask students to collect examples of headlines (from news sites, social media feeds, and so on). Choose a few examples that present information in straightforward, declarative fashion and ask students to note how they're similar in structure, tone, or message.
2. Choose a few parody headlines from sites such as *The Onion*. Parody works by combining the conventions of a genre with disparate material for comedic effect.

---

14. A listicle is an article in list form, as in "This Year's 10 Best Grammar Memes" or "Eight Foolproof Ways to Spot a Liar."

Ask students to note how parodic examples follow the form of news headlines and how they deviate from expectations (i.e., why they're funny).
3. Next, have student groups work to develop legitimate headlines about recent school, local, or other relevant events, meeting the expectations of the previous examples.
4. Finally, ask groups to *skew* the headlines they've created to purposely convey an inaccurate, disingenuous, or misleading message.

Even mainstream news outlets are not above the sensationalism of clicks for profit. *USA Today* (2017) took some well-deserved criticism when reporting on remarks from NFL quarterback Tom Brady through their sports Twitter account. At the time, several of Brady's teammates had decided not to participate in the traditional White House visit for Super Bowl champions in protest of President Trump's policies. Here's what *USA Today* (2017) tweeted, along with a link to an article:

> Tom Brady says teammates should "put politics aside" when it comes to visiting the White House.

Wow, that sounds contentious and dramatic, a star QB directly calling out his colleagues. The related article, however, reports something quite different. While reflecting on scheduling issues that prevented him from attending a previous White House visit, Brady said:

> I'd been planning for months and couldn't get [to the White House] …. It really is a great experience. Putting politics aside, it never was a political thing. At least, it never was to me.
>
> (Fang, 2017)

We might ask students to consider why *USA Today* editors might purposefully mischaracterize Brady's comments. What would a more accurate headline have been? What does the tweet imply about the situation that might get readers to click the link for more details? In this case, *USA Today* distorted Brady's remarks in order to manufacture "heat" and drama. Moderate and reasonable comments about a complex situation aren't as entertaining as a made-up conflict between team members. In short, drama (real or not) generates clicks which generates more advertising revenue.

With Students…

1. Ask students to locate a few innocuous, run-of-the-mill headlines from news sites or social media feeds.
2. Next, tell them their task is to transform the headline into juicy clickbait. The trick here is not to outright lie, but to create a suggestive lure with enough scandal or drama to get a reader to click that link.

Simplistic Binaries Through Syntactic Forms

Ideally, schools prepare students to lead productive lives as adults, part of which involves dealing with complex personal and social problems that don't have easy or simple answers. Dealing with complexity is difficult![15] It can be much easier and comforting to rely on simplistic right-wrong notions, especially when complex thinking might lead a person to question long-held beliefs or the values of their community.

Unfortunately, social media often encourages simplistic thinking. The ease of memetic communication through one's feeds comes with necessary constraints: a short, punchy message must often be shorn of nuance or context to trigger a desired reaction. Consider the examples below:

- "America: love it or leave it."
- "It's better to die on your feet than live on your knees."
- "Veterans should get benefits before illegal immigrants. Share if you agree!"

These are all *simplistic binaries:*[16] statements that reduce complex ideas and debates into clear good/bad divisions. Even though two options are presented, there's obviously only one viable choice implied.[17] You can help students identify simplistic binaries based on their sentence structure, which may use:

- a simple or compound sentence form
- either/or, this-or-that, before-and-after, or cause-effect structures
- comparative adjective forms to establish relationships (e.g., harder, better, faster, stronger, etc.)

With Students…

Unpacking simplistic binaries from a neutral space can be a good way to consider statements that may carry a lot of cultural baggage for students. For instance, most students have probably heard the "love it or leave it" imperative, and some may generally agree with this statement. Assigned (or having located) a simplistic binary, student groups might consider the questions below in deconstructing the message and its implications:

- What might be a counter opinion (or counter example) for this statement?
- When might this statement be correct, and when might it be incorrect? When might it not be true?
- In what kind of context might a person reasonably disagree with this statement?
- What does the statement not consider? What does it possibly ignore?

Finally, groups can create counter-responses to these simplistic binaries that disrupt some of the rigid options in favor of more complexity, perhaps using humor or inclusivity as a tactic (as in "America: do something every day so people like living here more than they did yesterday").

---

15. As Helen Keller noted, "People don't like to think. If one thinks, one must reach conclusions. Conclusions are not always pleasant."
16. Simplistic binaries are sometimes known as "false dichotomies."
17. "Lead, follow, or get out of the way" is an example of a *simplistic ternary*, in which three oversimplified options exist.

Hedging, Generalizing, and Just Asking Questions

Hedging language is a useful rhetorical tool, allowing us to avoid absolute statements and inaccurate generalizations. Words such as *may, might, some, sometimes, most, many, can,* and *could* help modify statements and make them palatable to a wider audience. Consider the sentence below:

> Dr. Seuss's books contain racial stereotypes.

We can dial up the absolute quality of this statement by adding *all of* as the first words (which would also not surprisingly dial up the controversy). Another option to open the sentence, *some of*, is a much more moderate foray into the topic. Practical practice with hedging language can have immediate benefits for young people, helping to maintain relationships and convey moderation. Few of us appreciate direct and unmitigated criticism ("your breath is terrible") when a gentler approach could get the same idea across ("sometimes your breath is less than fresh").

Alas, misinformation creators and other manipulators will employ both hedging and generalization for manipulative or dishonest purposes, as the examples below demonstrate:

1. "Source: Series of wildfires on the West Coast may be 'coordinated and planned' attack" (Flanagan, 2020; Gallagher, 2021)
2. "Critical Race Theory teaches our kids that all white people are racist, and if you are black and brown you can't be racist because somehow you are oppressed!" (Harriot, 2021)

Example 1 above is subtly insidious. The use of "may" as a hedging word creates a false sense of plausibility, as proving a negative (i.e., establishing conclusively that arson isn't the cause) is near impossible. To be clear, there is no evidence whatsoever of coordinated arson as the cause of the 2020 wildfire outbreak in the American West (and the supposed source is phony too), but by the time this headline was debunked, many thousands had seen and spread this lie online. This tactic of propelling a lie towards virality before it can be extinguished by the truth—a kind of linguistic arson in itself—is yet another common rhetorical trick of conspiracists. We see it again in Example 2, which spreads a bogus definition of Critical Race Theory using absolute language ("all") and generalizations, along with a tone of outrage.

A similar tactic might be called "just asking questions." We're all familiar with *leading questions*[18] and *loaded questions*[19] from TV courtroom dramas. Both are forms of "complex questions" that presuppose facts not yet established and serve as a platform for unfounded implications extending from the inquiry. Even ridiculous propositions can be granted legitimacy through this approach. The question "Are UFOs partly responsible for global warming?" at least partially admits the proposition that *aliens might be to be blame* as legitimate. Questions also seem naturally less accusatory than assertions, which

---

18. "Isn't it true, Mr. Smith, that you've always had a hatred for authority?"
19. "Ms. Jones, how long has it been since your last episode of shoplifting?"

make them subtle tools for shaping how an audience understands the grounds of a topic. Consider the following:

- "Is the Liberal Media Helping to Fuel Terror?"
- "Is Antifa Starting the Wildfires?"
- "When Will Senator Schumer Tell the Truth?"

Notice how each of these questions assumes a) that the topic itself warrants legitimate discussion, and thus b) the premises suggested *could* be true. These kinds of questions trade on fears and anxieties, creating a tableau suggesting that things are not what they seem. Before a conversation even begins, the landscape of what is real (or could be real) has been redefined.

With Students...

We can help students gain critical distance with social media-based headlines, accusations, questions, and assertions with prompts such as the following:

- How does the statement/question define what is real or worth considering?
- How are hedging words or generalizations used to convey plausibility?
- What role does a tone of outrage play in a statement or question?

This last question gets at an important and under-examined area of language arts: the emotional power of statements that can quickly trigger our biases and fears, which can sideline our ability to assess claims and judge the evidence (because we're just so outraged!). Humans tend to be emotional creatures prone to prejudice and tribal beliefs that are remarkably immune to facts and evidence; recent research suggests that the sharing of bogus news is a key facet of partisan polarization (Osmundsen et al., 2021). Part of what we might do as English teachers is help young people understand their own affiliations and possible biases, so that they, in turn, can understand their possible emotional trigger points (Crovitz & Moran, 2020).

Alliteration

Alliteration is an extremely common tactic in news presentation, as repeated sounds in nearby words can produce a rhythmic and memorable quality. The downside of alliterative prose, however, is familiar to any lyrical poet: when we choose words based on their sounds rather than the best fit for meaning, we're necessarily hemmed in by our options, and we risk distorting reality. Examples of alliterative headlines, taglines, chyrons,[20] and slogans aren't necessarily a purely digital phenomenon, but they have a bumper-sticker ability to lodge in our minds and are well adapted for viral distribution in online networked spaces.

Fox News, for instance, demonstrates a kind of mastery with alliterative headlines. Anytime the Democratic Party is grappling with some internal issue, we can expect to

---

20. A chyron is the caption at the bottom of the screen that often accompanies a news report or commentary.

see Fox News attach a "Dems in Disarray" title to the story.[21] Students might be on the lookout for how terms such as "Cancel Culture"[22] and slogans such as "Heritage Not Hate" (in support of Confederate iconography) and "Jobs Not Mobs" act as alliterative signifiers with slippery definitions. Just what is meant by these phrases is often mystified, and useful work can explore what we might otherwise skip past.

With Students…

The sound-bite slogans discussed above deserve a close reading. Questions such as these can get you started:

- What does "cancelling" imply? What other words might be more accurate?
- What kinds of behavior or statements are deserving of "cancellation," if any?
- Is public censure a new concept? If not, how should we consider other moments of cultural change in the United States, in which previous assumptions (e.g., voting permitted for men only) were questioned?
- Whose heritage is represented by the Confederate flag? Whose isn't?
- To what degree can symbols associated with certain concepts be rehabilitated with words?

Alliterative sloganeering may have found its zenith in "Stop the Steal," a term that rhetoric professor Mercieca (2021) calls a "condensation symbol" in its power to capture a variety of related concepts, trigger an audience's basic values, and spur listeners to action. Devised by Trump advisor Roger Stone and used to fan popular support for overturning the results of the 2020 U.S. presidential election (Hayden, 2020), the phrase was ideal for virality over veracity by

- identifying a common crime familiar to all (a supposed "steal")
- providing a de facto assumption of truth (pretending there is no dispute about the crime)
- characterizing the crime as ongoing and thus possibly preventable (the present tense of "stop")
- supplying an imperative call to action ("stopping" a crime)
- positioning sympathetic listeners in a righteous role (as crime stoppers)
- packaging the message with alliterative punch and rhythm (the double consonance of "st" in a simple spondaic trimeter suitable for chanting)
- linguistically echoing earlier tribalized slogans (such as "Build the Wall," "Back the Blue," and "Lock Her Up")

---

21. While the word "Democrats" is routinely shortened to "Dems," there isn't a similar plural abbreviation for Republicans. The best that left-leaning channels might attempt is a play on "GOP," as in "**GOP**roblems." Fox News' right-wing leanings preclude equal alliterative shorthand emphasizing Republican disagreements.
22. Perhaps most absurdly employed by trainer Bob Baffert in defense of Medina Spirit, the racehorse that won the 2021 Kentucky Derby but subsequently failed a drug test. We might even say that Baffert's defense—that the accusation of doping was the result of "cancel culture" run amok—is an apt example of [a horse] jumping the shark.

You can help students identify and analyze such slogans for these kinds of assumptions. And, as Hobbs (2020) would advocate (and we detail later), you can help students develop their own mastery of propaganda for their own purposes, including counternarratives and petitions for inclusivity, justice, and equity.

Weaponization of Language

As we've seen, any text that can convey ideas quickly—memes and slogans included—can be weaponized to deliver lies and disinformation. If you're repulsed by this behavior, we understand, as it basically contradicts everything we learned as children about using language for kindness, fairness, and truth. Unfortunately, these distortions are a modern digital reality. Division and polarization are goals of powerful entities, and while social chaos can obviously take an explicit form (as in the long-term protests and almost nightly rioting in Portland instigated by far-left groups and anarchists during 2020), more subtle means of disruption proliferate online.

The internet has become the modern home of coordinated disinformation efforts and conspiracy theories. Helping students understand the origin, intent, and impact of these phenomena through close analysis can transform an English language arts classroom. Suddenly we're talking about the interplay of language, story, truth, and reality in ways that have immediate relevance for the future of a democratic citizenry.

Hostile foreign states[23] have complex and ongoing operations to spread disinformation through social media and networking sites, propagating conspiracy theories on a variety of topics: COVID vaccines, 5G technology, the causes of wildfires, and really any current news story that can be exploited. Domestic conspiracy operations such as QAnon have built a modern mythology about the "deep state" and its evil machinations. These ideas have gained traction among many Americans.

With Students...

We might begin by asking students to ponder the point and purpose of conspiracy theories in general:

- What are some conspiracy theories that you know about, and how do these stories conflict with commonly accepted truth?
- What might be attractive about a story that supposedly reveals a secret truth?
- Who might be susceptible to such stories?

One common reaction to online conspiratorial content is a kind of perplexed shrug: *who can say what motivates people to spread lies and misinformation? Some people just like causing chaos.*[24] We can help students understand conspiracy theories as part of an intentional broader goal:

---

23. Notably Russia, as made clear in the conclusions of the Mueller Report and in subsequent reporting.
24. An analogous mystification sometimes occurs in references to specific U.S. political adversaries (e.g., Saddam Hussein and other dictators referred to as "monsters" or "madmen"), with the effect of halting any complex discussion about practical interests, international relationships, and realpolitik dynamics.

- Why would foreign adversaries seek to spread disinformation through American social media?
- Why would foreign Russian operatives pose as U.S. citizens with strong political opinions?
- Why would phony social media accounts push ideas and opinions that reinforce stereotypes and suspicions?
- Who benefits when Americans are pitted against one another?

While comprehensive strategies for detecting "fake news" are beyond the scope of this book, any sustained discussion of how the narratives take root inevitably begins with language, from clickbait headlines that trigger our biases to polarizing slogans designed to oversimplify complexity.

WHAT ARE LITERACIES FOR?

How are truth, power, language, and literacy connected? What examples are worth studying?

At its most central, language is at the center of both human liberation and control. Any conversation about grammar should eventually lead (if we keep talking, that is) to a discussion of power: how it's gained or lost, how it's maintained, how people use it in various ways, who has access to it and who doesn't, whose version of events matter. If we don't engage students in such topics, if we simply recite rules and assign practice exercises as the extent of grammar's relevance, we run the risk of turning language study into trivia. A digitally connected, always-on world amplifies the gulf between the compelling crises of modern life and the traditional busywork of typical classrooms. We can and must do better as language arts teachers.

REFERENCES

Aldridge, B. (2021, May 17). 'Absolutely bogus.' Some in GOP slam Republican attempts to downplay Capitol attack. *McClatchy DC Bureau*. https://www.mcclatchydc.com/news/politics-government/article251454943.html

Barry, D., McIntire, M., & Rosenberg, M. (2021, May 28). 'Our president wants us here': The mob that stormed the Capitol. *The New York Times*. https://www.nytimes.com/2021/01/09/us/capitol-rioters.html

Brauer, L., & Clark, C. T. (2008, July). The trouble is English: Reframing English studies in secondary schools. *English Education*, 40(4), 293–313.

Brewster, J. (2021, April 26). Fox news apologizes for airing misleading graphic accusing Biden of wanting to curb meat consumption. *Forbes*. https://www.forbes.com/sites/jackbrewster/2021/04/26/fox-news-apologizes-for-airing-misleading-graphic-accusing-biden-of-wanting-to-curb-meat-consumption/?sh=3437ffeb4392

Bump, P. (2021, April 20). How the first statement from Minneapolis police made George Floyd's murder seem like George Floyd's fault. *The Washington Post*. https://www.washingtonpost.com/politics/2021/04/20/how-first-statement-minneapolis-police-made-george-floyds-murder-seem-like-george-floyds-fault/

Crovitz, D., & Moran, C. (2020). Analyzing disruptive memes in an age of international interference. *English Journal*, 109(4), 62–69.

Fang, K. (2017, February 14). USA Today criticized for misleading headline on Tom Brady's White House quotes. *Awful Announcing*. https://awfulannouncing.com/nfl/usa-today-criticized-for-misleading-headline-tom-bradys-quotes-regarding-patriots-white-house-quotes.html

Ferguson, K. (Writer and Director). (2021). *Everything is a remix*. [Everything is a remix. [Video]. https://www.everythingisaremix.info/

Flanagan, A. (2020, September 12). Arson arrests made across the west coast as fires rage on. *Law Enforcement Today*. https://www.lawenforcementtoday.com/sources-series-of-wildfires-may-be-coordinated-and-planned-attack/

Gallagher, E. (2021, July 7). Misidentification: How the #Antifafires rumor caught on like wildfire. *Media Manipulation Casebook*. https://mediamanipulation.org/case-studies/misidentification-how-antifafires-rumor-caught-wildfire?s=09

Harriot, M. (2021, March 30). Why white people hate critical race theory, explained. *The Root*. https://www.theroot.com/why-white-people-hate-critical-race-theory-explained-1846578811

Harvey, L., & Palese, E. (2018). #NeverthelessMemesPersisted: Building critical memetic literacy in the classroom. *Journal of Adolescent & Adult Literacy*, 62(3), 259–270.

Hayden, M. E. (2020, Nov 6). Far right resurrects Roger Stone's #StopTheSteal during vote Count. *Southern Poverty Law Center*. https://www.splcenter.org/hatewatch/2020/11/06/far-right-resurrects-roger-stones-stopthesteal-during-vote-count

Hobbs, R. (2020). Mind over media: Propaganda education for a digital age. https://www.mindovermedia.us/

Jones, R. H., & Hafner, C. A. (2021). *Understanding digital literacies: A practical introduction* (2nd ed.). Routledge. https://doi.org/10.4324/9780203095317

Levin, S. (2017, February 6). Fake news for liberals: Misinformation starts to lean left under Trump. *The Guardian*. https://www.theguardian.com/media/2017/feb/06/liberal-fake-news-shift-trump-standing-rock

Mercieca, J. [Jennifer Mercieca]. (2021, May 19). *"Stop the Steal" is a condensation symbol* [Tweet]. Twitter. https://twitter.com/jenmercieca/status/1395009262888366081

Osmundsen, M., Petersen, M. B., & Bor, A. (2021, May 13). How partisan polarization drives the spread of fake news. *Brookings*. https://www.brookings.edu/techstream/how-partisan-polarization-drives-the-spread-of-fake-news/

Singer, P. W., & Brooking, E. T. (2019). *LikeWar: The weaponization of social media* (Reprint ed.). Mariner Books.

Swenson, A. (2021, April 26). Biden climate plans don't include red meat restrictions. *APnews.com*. https://apnews.com/article/fact-checking-813700209067

USA TODAY Sports. (2017, February 14). [Tweet]. Twitter. https://twitter.com/usatodaysports/status/831529824997036033

Watts, C. (2019). *Messing with the enemy: Surviving in a social media world of hackers, terrorists, Russians, and fake news* (Reprint ed.). Harper Paperbacks.

Wylie, C. (2019). *Mindf*ck: Cambridge Analytica and the plot to break America*. Random House.

SECTION III
Counter the Narrative

CHAPTER 6

Using Digital Language to Change the World

One of the most challenging tasks teachers face is balancing the demands of the curriculum with the interests of students. Way back in 1902, John Dewey[1] wrote about this tension, arguing that, "any significant problem involves conditions that for the moment contradict each other" (p. 3). Then, as now, competing voices struggled to shape educational policies: some advocating for standards and traditional ways of knowing and learning, others advocating for children following their own interests. Dewey felt that a delicate balance must be preserved. He acknowledged the ultimate purpose of an American education—to instill and uphold democratic ideals—while at the same time insisting that a student's interests must be taken into account.

Most know that students' knowledge and expertise, anchored in their unique worlds, is an effective and engaging way to teach. At the same time, teachers are bound by standardized curricula, state-mandated testing, and other conventional expectations. It's a tough challenge doing justice to both.

The digital landscape, however, can help us out. A careful blend of technology, multimodality, and English language arts content can help balance the demands of the curriculum with the interests of students. In the first section of this book, we advocate for capitalizing on the affordances of technology to teach grammar and language rhetorically. In the second section, we focus on the rhetoric of digital language and the importance of moving our students (and ourselves) toward a more critical digital literacy. Ultimately, we think becoming better writers, savvier consumers, and more engaged citizens is a means to an end.

We think it's a way to change the world.

In this section, we provide a map for using language, rhetoric, and technology toward social action and, hopefully, social change. These projects can be integrated into your existing units, perhaps serving as a summative assessment that focuses on justice, equity, or activism. We advocate for teachers to take on the role of teacher-facilitators, something akin to what King (1993) called "the guide on the side" rather than the "sage on stage." When students are fluent in rhetorical language use (Part 1) and critical digital literacy (Part 2), they can take on projects that might make a difference in their own lives and in their communities (where you are now, Part 3). At its most basic, the work

---

1. Dewey is among the most influential educational reformers. Writing during the early part of the 20th century, he is best known for *The School and Society* (1900) and *The Child and the Curriculum* (1902).

students do in the classroom should *matter* to them and others. The projects that follow offer opportunities to counter prevailing narratives, encouraging students to embrace the language and world-changing potential of digital spaces.

The first four projects ask students to analyze and create texts across a wide spectrum; topics include celebrity social media accounts, online disinformation campaigns, manufactured personas in the entertainment field, and the challenge of changing conventional attitudes toward engineered forms of food. All engage students in critical and creative responses based on real-world texts and involve important issues of power, identity, and equity.

The fifth project harnesses students' interest in social media sites to help them take action in their community and effect change. This project uses the principles of social action advocated by the National Writing Project.[2] These include (1) considering *what* issues are of concern to students; (2) understanding *why* the problem exists; (3) considering *how* action can help change things; (4) taking the *action*; and (5) *reflecting* on what was done and what changed (Berden et al, 2006, p. 9). Figure 6.1 describes this process.

Although the example we provide for the fifth project advocates for environmental change, this work can be adapted to focus on social change or justice in any number of fields. The process for taking social action is iterative, often leading to more questions than final answers, and it's important to note that school-based social action projects face unique constraints of time and focus. Your students may have limited opportunities to judge the impact of their efforts beyond the classroom. Even so, experimenting with such work can set the stage for the future. Change is often slow and hard-won, requiring long-term vision, determination, and persistence. To stick with such commitments in our day-to-day lives, we have to care deeply about what we're doing. Projects that are student-centered and student-led, that tap into passions and interests, that activate their sense of justice and fairness, can help prepare students for meaningful lives as democratic citizens, in whatever form that might take.

Finally, the last project (detailed in Chapter 7) focuses on linguistic and cultural appropriation in digital spaces; we provide a framework for exploring this important topic with your students in practical ways. We fully acknowledge this as a potentially controversial and slippery subject, requiring deep discussion. You know your students and your teaching context best, and we encourage you to take up these ideas in ways suitable for your situation.

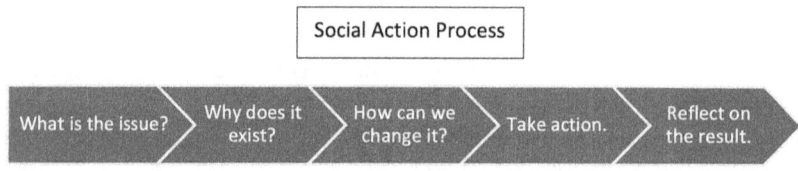

Figure 6.1 Process for Taking Social Action

---

2. The National Writing Project is a non-profit organization that promotes the teaching of writing and the development of writing teachers at all grade levels. See https://www.nwp.org.

All of the projects included here can be adjusted for student-inspired discovery. Much of this work is messy—we don't include rubrics and there are no prescribed formulas. But we believe that students and teachers, prepared with strategies for how to use grammar and rhetoric through technology, can effect real change. We invite you to make these ideas your own.

PROJECT #1: SOCIAL MEDIA CELEBRITY ACCOUNTS AS TEXTS[3]

General Task

This project asks students to analyze a particular celebrity's social media account for how it functions as an ongoing, evolving text. In so doing, they'll consider how the account—through posts, messages, images, and other content and features—serves to define or reinforce the celebrity's persona and seeks to develop a specific relationship with fans and followers. More broadly, students will assess how the feed enacts a version of *authenticity* and reproduces, amplifies, questions, or subverts particular generalizations and stereotypes.

Background

While social media platforms and applications have transformed our personal lives in numerous ways, the affordances of platforms such as Instagram, Twitter, and TikTok have also been embraced by business, entertainment, and corporate interests. Notably, companies and celebrities have recognized the value of social media spaces in curating branded identities and communicating in ways that convey authenticity to customers, fans, and followers.

Celebrities (including actors, singers, athletes, YouTube personalities, and social influencers) are no longer limited to static, branded personas maintained at a distance from audiences. Social networking platforms mean that famous figures can cultivate a more personal kind of interaction with fans, posting personal images and messages and responding directly to followers in a forum that conveys intimacy and connection. Arguably, creating and maintaining a persona based on "authenticity" —coming across as a real person, basically—is an increasingly important means of building a following and monetizing fame.

We can view such social media channels as complex, constructed texts engaged in the production, distribution, and reception of meaning. In essence, these accounts tell stories which are at least partially inflected by ongoing interaction with an engaged audience. Depending on one's persona, this story may draw upon specific generalities and stereotypes—or it may challenge or subvert such generalities. For example, both Taylor Swift and Morgan Wallen are stars associated with country music (though Swift's cultural imprint now extends beyond this genre). How these figures use their social media channels to maintain specific personas and tell the story of themselves, however, may involve quite different strategies. In a sense, such channels are a useful example of

---

3. Thanks to current English teacher and former Kennesaw State University student Morganne Biddle for developing this idea.

modern propaganda as Hobbs (2020) defines it: campaigns that influence particular audiences with specific and intentional messaging.

The Specific Context

For this project, students will select a famous person with a large social media following (a singer, actor, rapper, athlete, influencer, or someone similar). They will examine this person's social media accounts to create an analysis of

- the specific persona that this celebrity portrays to their following, and
- how this person attempts to represent authenticity or relatability to followers through specific language choices

Students can follow these steps:

1. As a class, students will examine and analyze several examples of celebrity accounts for how they use language and images to create and maintain a specific persona. The goal is to analyze the texts on these platforms—photos, posts, responses to fan comments, and similar content—for how they tell a story about who this person is. For instance, the class might consider together the Instagram accounts of Taylor Swift, Jojo Siwa,[4] and Trae Young[5]. These accounts each present a curated picture of a celebrity, with images chosen to convey a specific identity, lifestyle, mood, and perspective.
2. Next, they will choose a person with whom they are familiar—perhaps someone they follow—to perform a careful analysis of how this famous figure creates the sense of an authentic relationship with fans. The following list of questions can help in thinking about a social media profile as a complex text.

    - Who or what are the subjects of their posts, images, and videos?
    - Are there any specific posts that stand out to you? Why?
    - Are the posts mostly about their personal lives, their careers, or something else?
    - Do they interact with other people? If so, who and how?
    - Are their photos super-filtered, or more natural-looking? Are they candid or posed?
    - What are their captions like? Does it sound like they're directly speaking to their audience, or not so much?
    - What does their profile picture say about them?
    - How do they describe themselves in their bio?
    - Do they use a lot of hashtags and tags, and if so, what is notable about their choices?
    - Do they post advertisements? If so, how are these products connected to the image they've curated? How do they endorse or promote particular products or services through their posts or images?

---

4. A singer, dancer, and YouTube personality.
5. An NBA all-star.

3. In particular, consider the specific language choices—including particular grammatical moves—and how these choices might

   - Convey authenticity
   - Build community with followers
   - Create a space that is inclusive to some degree (Who is included? Who isn't?)
   - Tell a story about the kind of person the celebrity really is

4. Next, what kinds of generalizations, stereotypes, and assumptions do students notice on these accounts? They might think about depictions of the following.

   - Typical followers: Who are they and what do they like?
   - Common activities and social situations
   - Places, locations, and regions
   - Political and social opinions or values expressed

   Overall, students should think both about who and what is depicted, and who and what isn't (and why).

5. Finally, they can use a digital platform or space to create a multimodal project/presentation that presents what they have found. They can include edited screenshots of specific examples from the subject's social media accounts along with a detailed analysis of what these examples demonstrate or suggest. They should try to draw some broad conclusions about how these texts work as ongoing stories about the celebrity's persona.

PROJECT #2: DISINFORMATION TAKEDOWN

General Task

This project asks students to choose and analyze a form of internet-based disinformation—a conspiracy theory, basically—for how people use social media and networking to convey concepts that question established reality.

Background

The pioneering internet thinker and philosopher Jaron Lanier (2019) has consistently raised probing criticisms of social networking and digital media ecosystems. In his books,[6] Lanier argues that the current version of our online experiences—manifested and channeled through a few gigantic internet corporations—is a threat to privacy, individual fulfillment, and social cohesion. Indeed, an uncritical view of any technology means that the constraints of that technology may remain unexamined and its long-term ramifications and dangers invisible.

Take, for instance, the recent proliferation of conspiracy theories in American culture. Communities in pre-internet times certainly contained a few people or groups with beliefs that we might generously call "discrepant" in light of commonly

---

6. Namely *You Are Not a Gadget* (2011) and *Ten Arguments for Deleting Your Social Media Accounts Right Now* (2019).

accepted norms, such as Flat Earth theory, chemtrails, Illuminati-related millennium-long alternate histories of secret global governments, or any of a range of beliefs not supported by facts. But back then, these folks remained outliers in society. They were few and far between, and while they might subscribe to underground newsletters or publications that promoted these strange ideas, there simply weren't enough people in the average town[7] believing in such fictions to have much of an effect or impact on mainstream society.

In the social media internet age, all of this has changed.

Now, anyone can find a community online easily. The affordances of social media—easy sharing of information, algorithmically determined based on what we've shared, clicked on, or liked—means that ideas previously considered ridiculous are easily recast to seem legitimate and subsequently amplified through one's networks. Conspiracies previously limited to a few outsiders thirty years ago are now being mainlined into our lives, mixed into "news feeds" and presented as factual. The foundational concepts of modern civilization (scientific agreement, the credibility of field-based experts, the democratic rule of law, long-established social custom, shared facts) are called into question by millions of our fellow citizens. Now, don't get us wrong. We love questioning facts and conceptions of truth; in fact, we believe doing so is an important component of democracy and personal growth. But when information that is easily proven false through multiple reliable and scientific channels is instead taken as fact, we have to stop and reconsider our direction as a society and country.

The Specific Context

For this project, students will locate a specific example of disinformation[8] or conspiracy theorizing and examine how it spreads across a social media channel. They can choose a common and widespread phenomenon—such as Flat Earthers or the New World Order and the Denver Airport—or focus on a local example with which they are familiar.

To do this work, students should follow these general steps.

1. Determine a particular focus. The Media Manipulation Casebook (n.d.)[9] (https://mediamanipulation.org/) provides extended examples of how broad conspiracy theories and disinformation are purposefully amplified across media platforms. They might also be familiar with topics from their own social networking feeds or be aware of a specific local phenomenon that they'd like to investigate.
2. Research the phenomenon: read news articles, examine specific examples of how this material is spread, and consider why it might stoke people's fears or suspicions.
3. To accompany this research, students may want to consider why this focus continues to be spread on social media sites. Why do people want to believe this information? Does it encourage in-group or out-group status? With what groups might it do so?

---

7. Cities, meanwhile, have long provided inclusive community and refuge for those considered different.
8. Disinformation is false material that is intentionally packaged and spread to mislead others. In contrast, *misinformation* does not necessarily involve intent. We're often misinformed on various topics out of ignorance or simple error; disinformation, meanwhile, is a purposeful attempt to deceive.
9. Hobbs' Mind Over Media site (https://www.mindovermedia.us/) is also a possible resource.

4. Screenshot[10] social media posts as examples to analyze. They should be looking for how false stories are presented as factual, and how audiences are manipulated or encouraged to spread this material further.
5. Organize their analysis on an online platform as a "takedown" of false information. Be sure to provide:

    a. Background and context about the specific situation or event
    b. The actual facts about the situation or event
    c. Examples of distorted facts advancing conspiracy narratives
    d. Explanation of the language choices in these examples: how are grammar concepts used rhetorically to sway readers and viewers?

6. Finally, students can create several memes that speak back to this disinformation with accurate remedies. They should use suitable meme templates to emphasize and amplify actual established facts, settled knowledge, and accepted truths in an effort to counter bogus stories and messaging.

PROJECT #3: SHIFTING FOOD PERCEPTIONS

General Task

This project challenges students to draw upon various grammar concepts (see Section 1) in designing a multimodal campaign to shift public perceptions about an unfamiliar or new food item. The broader task is to convince consumers to consider changing their diets—how might they be persuaded to consider new types of food that help address various resource-based challenges of the future?

Background

The benefits of new technologies are often obvious, especially when they make our lives easier or more convenient. For every iPhone or Alexa or Roomba, however, there have also been inventions that required some serious persuasion for skeptical customers to consider. Indoor flushing toilets were initially a hard sell for people accustomed to the pungent aroma of an outhouse—after all, who would want that persistent odor *inside their house?* Homeowners had to be convinced that the benefits of installing such a contraption indoors outweighed the drawbacks. Similarly, when microwave oven technology became a commercial reality in the 1960s, the industry faced a significant challenge: how to convince atomic-era homemakers that adding a radiation-producing appliance to the kitchen was a safe choice. Again, this involved amplifying the technology's affordances while reassuring customers and reducing their fears.

Similar challenges face food manufacturers attempting to sell "new" items to the American public. Sushi, tofu, soy milk, kombucha, kefir, and similar products—all fairly common today in many grocery stores—needed specific advertising campaigns to educate consumers and shift attitudes. The fact that these items are now unremarkable on

---

10. If you use any screenshots as part of your research, be sure to anonymize individual identities. Remove or obscure names and do not include photos of individuals.

store shelves is the result of focused campaigns[11] that were designed to shift conceptions of a product and, just as importantly, adjust how we think of ourselves and what we consider normal. Similarly, food industries of the future (e.g., cultured lab-grown meat, insect proteins as viable food additives) will need story experts to help reshape public consciousness about what is typical and acceptable.

Every business—particularly small- to medium-sized local operations—needs astute writers and storytellers to distinguish themselves from competitors. Businesses and organizations win new customers in part by listening to and understanding their current customers and then crafting new stories that simultaneously appeal to and educate potential customers about new products.

The Specific Context

For this project, students will research the long-term food challenges facing the globe, and choose a specific future-oriented food product that addresses an environmental, health-based, or social concern. Their choice should be a product that is likely to challenge the dietary conventions of the average consumer, and their primary task will be to turn something that may seem initially strange into a normal option.

Students might focus on foods such as the following:

- Fungus-based meat substitutes
- Plant-based seafood (i.e., "alt-fish")
- Lab-grown cultured meat
- Insect protein (in powdered form)
- Algae-derived milk
- A similar new food product that seeks to address sustainability issues associated with conventional food production

Their specific work is to create materials that will accompany a particular product as it's presented to the public. This work includes the following steps:

1. Choosing a particular alternate food focus.
2. Researching the specific alternate food industry related to your choice. This step means understanding the *problem addressed* by this alternative food (e.g., environmental issues with factory or industrial farming, the negative health effects of current food choices, increasing population demands on resources, animal welfare concerns, etc.) as well as the *challenges faced* in marketing this new food to the public.
3. Creating a marketing plan for the product, which includes

   a. Brainstorming and selecting possible names the product
   b. Doing the same for a product slogan
   c. Drafting possible designs for the product logo, label, and packaging, including color scheme, fonts, imagery, and messaging

---

11. Campaigns that created positive narratives about the food item aimed at specific audiences.

4. Designing a launch for the product, which might include

   a. Several TikToks that generate interest in the product and direct interested viewers to a webpage for more detail
   b. A webpage that welcomes interested consumers and is organized to provide engaging details about the product with headings and welcoming, pleasant imagery and graphics

5. A one-page "sell sheet" that includes clear information about the product—including appropriate images, background information, and persuasive copy—for use with potential grocery store accounts
6. A summary of the project, in which they explain the rationale behind their choices

At each step of the creative process, students will need to draw upon their knowledge of the practical use of various grammatical concepts, likely including but not limited to the following:

- Various sentence forms (including sentence fragments) for effect
- Colons to provide emphasis
- Hyphens to convey new, combined, or hybrid qualities
- Adjectival phrases (e.g., "deliciously exotic!") in marketing materials

PROJECT #4: MANUFACTURING ENTERTAINMENT PERSONAS

General Task

In this project, students will consider how characters and personas are created and maintained within particular entertainment fields. After assessing the dynamics of the identities common in a chosen context, students will then create and pitch a new character or persona that somehow expands or challenges status quo expectations.

Background

Mass media entertainment is often driven by stories, and stories of course have characters. We're all familiar with characters from popular literary and film texts—from Harry Potter to Star Wars to the Marvel Cinematic Universe—and we understand how character dynamics are crucial to dramatic plots and storytelling. But character development also extends to other fields of entertainment beyond fiction:

- **Professional wrestling** features many characters with elaborate backstories and attributes that contribute to ongoing stories (of feuds, alliances, triumphs, defeats, and vengeance) with many ongoing dimensions and chapters. Wrestling characters of past eras often represented simplistic stereotypes, especially of non-white ethnicities (e.g., the Iron Sheik, Mr. Fuji, Kamala the Ugandan Giant, etc.) and non-hetero orientations (Adrian Adonis). While the genre remains heavily skewed toward representations of conventional masculinity, modern characters feature more diversity and complexity in their personas.

- **Reality TV shows** often rely on strategic editing (along with strong personalities) to create drama, intrigue, and conflict. While these shows feature actual people, many participants take on or develop particular roles as dramatic characters, depending on the particular genre. It's not uncommon for reality show participants to use their newfound fame (as a heartbroken bachelor, a scheming vixen, a "bad boy," etc.) to launch acting or celebrity careers.
- **Popular spectator sports** and team affiliations often depend on historical narratives (the fateful lore of a long-struggling team finally finding redemption), inter-squad rivalries (between two teams with "bad blood"), and personal grudges or competition between players that provides added tension, drama, and interest. Mass media sports coverage—dependent on advertising revenue and thus viewers to make money—purposely amplifies and contextualizes these stories and character elements for audiences in order to increase the narrative stakes.
- **Musical artist personas** can be a complex site of identity construction and depictions of authenticity. For instance, credibility is often an important feature of specific hip-hop, rap, and country genres, especially through genuine stories and personal histories that invoke rough beginnings and the struggle to overcome hardship. Recording companies may package or shape the image of specific artists (in effect participating in the creation or amplification of a character) to appeal to certain audiences, while perceived conflicts ("beefs" or feuds) between individuals might be woven into storylines and plots that continue across different tracks, albums, and other texts. Likewise, individual artists may position themselves to unsettle or challenge assumptions within the field. Hip hop artist Frank Ocean and rapper Lil Nas X, for instance, have both challenged the hetero-normative stereotypes of their genres to some acclaim.

Analysis of and creative experimentation with character development in these particular contexts can help students understand how language choices are part of a larger effort to drive narratives (for profit, fame, social justice, or other reasons).

The Specific Context

In this project, students will choose a specific entertainment field (such as professional wrestling, reality TV, spectator sports, a musical genre, or some other field) with which they are familiar,[12] focusing on a particular aspect that interests them about how individual stories and characters are created. They will then **develop a new character** to join this space, crafting a persona that in some way challenges the current storyline, structure, or status quo. Through this character, students will specifically take on an issue or stereotype that deserves more attention in this area.

In doing so, students should consider the following:

- The current "characters" that exist in the particular spaces and the stories in which they play a specific role
- How their character will fit within this space/universe/context in a believable way

---

12. We recommend that you highlight that students consider a genre with which they are familiar. This will ground the project in personal interest and help them avoid common stereotypes in less-familiar genres.

- How their character will shift the story within this space in ways that question, challenge, or rethink standard assumptions

Specifically, students will need to create the following to develop their character.

1. A backstory: how this person became who they are now, including key experiences that shaped the character
2. Specific identity markers (name, ethnicity, gender, etc.) and details about personal style and appearance
3. Values and vision: how this person sees the world, and how beliefs motivate particular actions now
4. Specific characteristics of your character's communication
5. Specific conflicts, challenges, or obstacles that this character is likely to encounter
6. Several stories, plots, or dramatic episodes in which this character will be involved

In terms of the final product, they will need to create the following for their character:

- Some kind of careful visual depiction with annotations that explain relevant details
- A character analysis that details the character concepts discussed above, focused on how this persona fits within and shifts the dynamics of their space
- A 45-second elevator pitch that uses vivid language and strategic language choices to gain attention and interest those who might greenlight your idea
- A summary of the current situation of the dramatic storylines and characters in their chosen context, followed by a reflection on the rationale for their choices.

PROJECT # 5: YOU'VE GOT THE WHOLE WORLD IN YOUR HANDS

General Task

This project asks students to use a five-step social action process to create a social media campaign designed to effect change. This gradual progression builds knowledge around digital tools and social media sites so that students can deliver a message to a wide audience outside the classroom. Students will have the opportunity to target an issue in their own community and consider the potential solutions for change.

Background

Those of us who are more than 40 years old can remember a time when DVD players and floppy discs were the essence of modern technology. Michelle likes to remind her students that even the car was seen as an affront to humanity by some when it first began replacing the horse and buggy. Likewise, our grandparents remember the uproar over the introduction of television and the subsequent fears that it would replace radio, and the familiarity of families sitting in a circle listening to their favorite program. Now, screens are ubiquitous, and TV has evolved from radio-signal networks broadcast to cable providers to internet streaming services providing on-demand content to all manner of devices. We can only imagine what's next.

Our students have grown up in this sliver of time with its unique technological advances, and they are likely to understand intuitively the world-changing potential of technology. This is *their* time, *their* moment to tackle the challenges of *their* generation, and tech-integrated projects in the ELA classroom can help. With or without us, young people now have the power to broadcast their ideas and use rhetoric for their own purposes. Ideally, we can help them with what they want to say.

The Specific Context

As teachers, we are used to setting the agenda for the day and directing students' learning. However, this project, which incorporates the social action process developed by the Centre for Social Action[13] in Leicester, England, relies on students as leaders, which helps "students acquire skills that [stretch] far beyond English and language arts to other disciplines" (Berden et al., 2006, p. 83). During this project, the teacher is positioned as the facilitator and coach, working alongside students who devise the specifics of the project and launch the action.

Social media sites, such as Instagram, Snapchat, Twitter, and Facebook,[14] supply the audience needed for the campaign. And digital tools, such as Canva, Google Jamboard, and Adobe Spark, can help with the development of the materials for the campaign. Everything presented here is "free."[15] All you need is internet-enabled devices, internet access, and student-led passion and interest.

First, keep in mind that projects anchored in "real world" advocacy require flexibility and patience. When National Writing Project teacher-leaders used social action principles in their classroom, they discovered that:

- Social action is a dynamic and unpredictable process.
- Such work takes time and can be messy—these projects often go beyond conventional assignment boundaries.
- Creators have to accept that they do not know what the outcomes will be; uncertainty is an important ingredient of the process.
- The teacher is never neutral. (Berden et al., 2006, p. 94)

Students may not see discernible results from their campaign. But they will have learned crucial skills for another more successful campaign later. Promoting change takes time and reflection, and this activity is a great place to begin.

The Five-Stage Process

1. Students can begin their social media campaign by asking **what** it is in the world (or their communities) that they want to change. Working in small groups, students can

---

13. This organization now goes by the name of the Centre for Social Justice. https://www.centreforsocialjustice.org.uk/
14. Although many people feel that Facebook users skew older, Facebook can provide a good outlet for a social media campaign attempting to reach a broad audience.
15. Nothing in life is truly "free," so it's worth a mention to students that the affordances of social media must be balanced by the constraints of advertising and capitalism. See Phase 2: Play or Be Played for guidance.

brainstorm about their passions and what affects their lives. For this example, we draw on ideas connected to environmental justice.

Break students into small groups and provide a large piece of poster paper or Flipchart paper and colored markers to each group—alternately, groups can record their thinking in a virtual document or a brainstorming app. On the board at the front of the room, write or project the following:

- What are some environmental issues or problems that we face?
- Are you concerned about the environment or another issue? What, specifically, concerns you?

Once students have exhausted the questions, direct them to an internet search, asking them to think about the following:

- What movies or TV shows reflect your beliefs and understandings?
- What images illustrate your beliefs and understandings?
- What websites reflect your beliefs and understandings? (Make sure the websites are legitimate and credible.)

Ask them to record their findings.

During this discovery and brainstorming stage, students work together to find a specific issue that really resonates with them. Students may disagree on a focal point but encourage them to reach a consensus. In the end, students should have settled on a single issue that they care about. Here are a few examples from a recent brainstorming session on climate change with Clarice's students:[16]

- The overuse of plastics and disposable items during the COVID-19 pandemic
- Paper face masks from COVID-19 littering sidewalks and parking lots
- Plastics that find their way into the ocean
- Too many fast-food containers made of Styrofoam and plastic

Post the Flipchart papers/posters around the classroom and conduct a gallery walk (also possible with virtual brainstorming); students jot down ideas, pictures, or comments that can further the group's thinking. Ask each group to read through the comments and discuss the issue some more. Is this really an issue that needs to be addressed?

2. The second stage involves understanding the root causes for the designated issue. **Why** is it a problem? A deep understanding of the cause will help students analyze and use the best language to effect change. An ineffective campaign might simply tell people, "Stop doing that!" Understanding the complexity of the problem and our own involvement with it can lead to a more successful tactic.

---

16. These students are particularly interested in environmental issues and climate change. Your students may not agree with the idea of climate change or prefer to examine a different issue. The steps would be the same.

Working in their small groups, ask students to conduct research on the internet about why their designated problem exists. Help them brainstorm previous solutions to their problem that may have failed. Ask them to come up with a list of "whys," both about why the problem exists and why other solutions have failed. These should be put on a Google Doc or Jamboard that is shared with the class. Each group will lead a discussion and seek input from their peers. If possible, project each group's Google Doc/Jamboard and have someone from the group take notes on the class discussion. Then, the original groups should reconvene and discuss the "whys" connected to their issue.

In our example, students decided to focus on the issue of Styrofoam and the overuse of plastics. In their research, they discovered that Styrofoam and plastics are relatively inexpensive and are good at containing liquids. Food packaged in plastic also tends to last longer than food packed in paper. Understanding the reasons why many merchants use these products helped the group devise a campaign that offered solutions instead of shame. Students also could have focused on merchants (whose use of these materials is related to products and services, profits, and costs) rather than just consumers.

3. Stage 3 asks students to begin brainstorming **solutions** to the problem. At this stage, every idea matters. Equity and openness are important in brainstorming because the process of airing all possible ideas without judgment helps uncover all possibilities. The goal is that this discussion leads students to a singular focus on their eventual campaign.

Students consider how their identified issue could be addressed, focusing on first organizing their message and considering its impact. Students should discuss potential messages that clarify their proposed solutions, recording them on the Google Doc/Jamboard from the previous step.

Next, ask students to create a short skit that illustrates the problem clearly for others. In the skit, there should be at least two roles: someone who is (for example) unfamiliar with the problems associated with Styrofoam or plastics and someone who works to explain the effects of these materials on the environment.[17] The point of the skit is for students to begin articulating how they will convince others to adopt a potential solution. Teachers should remind students about the rhetorical impacts of their language choices.

After formulating the skit, groups should perform them for the rest of the class. At the end of each, the group should solicit suggestions and input from their peers about their proposed solutions to the problem.

In our example, students devised a skit where a local restaurant worker packed a meal into a plastic or Styrofoam container and then handed it to a customer. After finishing the meal, the customer threw away the container. Another person observed this action and retrieved the container from the trash can. She then took the container, washed it

---

17. Clearly, the roles will be dependent upon the issue each student group chose. We are just sticking with the Styrofoam idea here in this example.

thoroughly, and repurposed it as a paint holder or a receptacle for her school supplies.[18] After the skit was completed, the group asked for more suggestions from their peers about other possible solutions.

A skit that focuses on producers and merchants may take a different direction, showing instead a merchant who answers the phone to receive a take-out order, asking the caller if they would like "cardboard or plastic." Picking up the order, the customer could thank the merchant for offering an alternative to plastic. After this skit is over, the actors could ask for more suggestions about alternatives to plastic and how merchants might be incentivized to use alternatives.

4. This stage involves taking **action** to solve the problem. It should be enacted only after the other stages have been thoroughly investigated. Without understanding the what, why, and how first, an action plan is doomed to fail. This stage requires internet-enabled devices and can be completed in or out of school.

Once students have settled on some specific solutions to the problem, they need to devise an action plan. This plan includes:

- **A memorable name** for the campaign. This name would be used on all digital sites, as well as any other handouts or campaign materials. (Example from our Styrofoam group: Eagerly Reuse All Styrofoam Every Day or ERASED. Students explained that the use of adverbs in this name helps encourage regular participation. The point is that students should find a name that reflects their goal.)
- **A slogan** for a social media campaign. (Example from our Styrofoam group: "Use it, don't lose it!"). This slogan should be repeated on all the materials in the campaign. It should use language in a way that attempts to persuade people to change.
- **Images** for the campaign that are taken either from Google images or created by the group. Students can use their phones to take pictures and then upload them to a shared Google site. Students also could draw pictures or cartoons; take a picture of these and upload them. (Example: Students took pictures of someone throwing away a Styrofoam carton and someone using a carton as a paint palette.)
- **Social media sites** created specifically for the campaign. Students can create an Instagram site, a Facebook page, a Twitter account, and/or a website. They should use their name consistently across all social media sites. (Example: Our ERASED group chose the handle "@Erased-it" and used this name on all of their sites.)

Once students have the elements of the campaign decided upon, it's time to get to work on pushing out their content to the world. Possibilities include the following:

- Memes that illustrate their point and then promote them with a hashtag that reflects their campaign's name. (Example: #erasedstyrofoam or #banplastics)
- An infographic (created with a site such as Canva) that provides simple steps to follow. (See Figure 6.2)

---

18. Interestingly, there are many websites with suggestions for repurposing Styrofoam take-out containers. See: https://get-green-now.com/reuse-styrofoam/

Figure 6.2 Example of an Infographic used in an Activism Campaign

- Original images that attempt to persuade people and repost them on Instagram
- Tweets featuring images and information that reflect their campaign's theme
- A website that includes solutions, ideas, and some of the research they gathered in the "why" phase, along with images
- A Pinterest board that has images reflecting positive ideas or solutions to the issue.
- Several TikTok videos that promote the campaign in creative ways
- A short video created with a phone-based app and uploaded to YouTube

Stage 4 could be extended for an entire academic year with students monitoring comments on social media, the number of followers, and the impact of the campaign.

It's important to note, too, that students could move their campaigns in a completely different direction, with a focus on merchants, suppliers, and companies. In this case, the students would research the cost of alternatives to Styrofoam or plastics and then target the campaign toward the larger players in order to convince them that they can attract more customers or add value to their business by offering more eco-friendly packaging. The point is that the campaigns—whatever direction they may take—are student-driven and the solutions to the problem are student-devised.

5. In the final stage, teacher-facilitators can sit down with each group and **reflect** on the project. Students should be invited to consider the successes and failures of their campaign and whether it should be restructured, relaunched, or changed completely.

After the social media campaign has run its course, groups should come together to ask themselves:

- What worked and why?
- What didn't work and why not?
- Are there ways to shift the language or the rhetoric to achieve more success?

This reflective process may result in more questions than answers. It also may spur students to want to try to effect change in a different way or on a different topic. Students should lead the way in thinking about the final outcome of the campaign and what role language, rhetoric, and digital tools played.

A personal reflection is a useful step before asking students to have a reflective conversation about the project's strengths and weaknesses. We like both FlipGrid and Padlet for this purpose. FlipGrid allows students to record their thoughts (up to 5 minutes) on a topic. Padlet is a digital bulletin board that allows students to pin their thoughts in a bulletin-board style format that others can read. Both tools can stimulate conversation and thinking in a public fashion.

With an emphasis on applied language use that might reverberate beyond the classroom, campaign-focused projects can help students grow in their capacity to use digital media in purposeful ways.

REFERENCES

Berden, K., Boulton, I., Eidman-Aadahl, E., Fleming, J., Gardner, L., Rogers, I., & Solomon, A. (2006). *Writing for a change: Boosting literacy and learning through social action.* Jossey-Bass.
Centre for Social Justice (2022). https://www.centreforsocialjustice.org.uk/
Dewey, J. (1902). *The child and the curriculum.* University of Chicago Press.
Hobbs, R. (2020). *Mind over media: Propaganda education for a digital age.* https://www.mindovermedia.us/
King, A. (1993). From sage on the stage to guide on the side. *College Teaching, 41*(1), 30–35. https://doi.org/10.1080/87567555.1993.9926781
Lanier, J. (2019). Ten arguments for deleting your social media accounts right now. Picador.
The Media Manipulation Casebook. (n.d.). https://mediamanipulation.org/

CHAPTER 7

Linguistic and Cultural Appropriation in Digital Contexts

In our politically divided world, where words, phrases, and their meanings are often placed in ideological camps, we want to begin this final section with explorations and definitions of what we mean by "linguistic and cultural appropriation." So let's begin with "appropriation," which is a pretty old word. And because we love language, we'll begin with its etymology:[1]

> Originating in the late 14th century, "the taking of (something) as private property." This word originally came from Late Latin *appropriationem* (nominative *appropriatio*) "a making one's own." From Latin *ad* (meaning "to") + *propriare* (meaning "take as one's own").
> (rephrased from Online Etymology Dictionary, www.etymonline.com)

So when appropriation happens, someone is taking something that doesn't belong to them. Check. Let's now dig into the words "linguistic" and "culture." Linguistic is easy: linguistic = language. Good. Moving right along.

Culture can be a little more slippery to define; however, like appropriation, we think its history gives a good lens to consider its current meaning. *Culture* came to English around the early 16th century with a meaning attached to farming. Its origins were Latin (*cultura, culturare*), meaning *growing* and *tend* respectively. In other words, the historical origins of *culture* are embedded in *growing* and *tending* food, which means sustenance, survival. Broader concepts of *culture* originate much later, in the early 19th century (Oxford Languages). For a more modern definition, we go to Dimen-Schein (1977) who defines culture as "the intangible symbols, rules, and values…that people use to define themselves" (p. 23). These symbols, rules, and values can include (but are certainly not limited to) things like language, food, clothes, and religion.

EXAMPLES: LINGUISTIC AND CULTURAL APPROPRIATION

Okay, so when we say "linguistic and cultural appropriation," we are talking about using language and culture that isn't your own. However, even that definition is

---

1. A fancy linguistic term meaning the word's history.

problematic: what about *loan words* and *language change*[2] and *cultural appreciation* and *cultural exchange* and all of the other ways we engage with and learn from cultures that aren't our own? Where is the line between legitimate use and stealing? Well, before we try a more apt definition, some examples might offer a wider lens before we zoom in on a more inclusive definition.

> Example 1: In 2019, two teenagers from Texas, Mya Johnson and Chris Cotter—both of whom are Black—created a dance to Cardi B's "Up." However, they weren't the ones who were invited to perform the dance live on the stage of *The Tonight Show with Jimmy Fallon*. That would be White TikTok personality Addison Rae, whose version of Johnson and Cotter's dance had gone viral. On the show, Rae performed a variety of dances, including the one choreographed by Mya and Chris[3] with no credit given (Asmelash, 2021).

> Example 2: In a spring 2016 fashion campaign, Italian designer Valentino featured African prints in his collection. Using only a few Black models and designing the White models' hair in cornrows, he labeled his African-inspired clothes "primitive" and "wild" (Hirsch, 2017). Such labeling can be considered condescending because it portrays African cultures and peoples as less civilized or "less advanced" than others. Criticism was immediate, and Valentino quickly tried to backtrack by flying photographers and models to Kenya for photoshoots that included people from the Maasai tribe; however, the damage had been done.

> Example 3: Madonna's 1990 hit "Vogue" is based on the style of a particular club culture; "voguing" as a look and dance originated in the ballroom scene of New York City in the 1980s, which "had an eclectic mix of performers from diverse backgrounds, mostly black and Latinx members of the LGBTQ community" (Saveriano, 2020, n.p.). Madonna learned voguing from two dancers familiar with the scene, hired those dancers for the music video, and brought them on tour with her. As "Vogue" ultimately became one of her biggest hits, Madonna arguably profited from using the artistic creativity of the LGBTQ community.[4]

So we see some themes in these examples. Individuals from a particular culture created something while those from another culture benefited from this creation. Let's go ahead and look at some examples of linguistic appropriation while we're here. Not to spoil the ending, but you'll see the same theme.

---

2. Can we say that English was committing linguistic appropriation by borrowing the Latin words in the etymological definitions above? (The answer is no, by the way, and you'll understand why by the end of this section.)

3. "Late Night with Jimmy Fallon" responded to the criticism by inviting the creators of the dances initially performed by Addison Rae. His guest list included "Mya Nicole Johnson and Chris Cotter, who created 'Up,' Dorien Scott of 'Corvette Corvette' fame, Fur-Quan Powell and Camyra Franklin of 'Laffy Taffy,' Adam Snyder, Nate Nale and Greg Dahl from 'Blinding Lights,' and Keara Wilson, who choreographed moves to 'Savage.'" (Garvey, 2021, n.p.).

4. This situation might be a good one to expand discussion in the classroom as to what cultural appropriation looks like. As Saveriano (2020) reminds us, Madonna was an early supporter of the LGBTQ community, and she gave credit to the ballroom scene for the dance; however, it was queer people of color that "allowed for that song and video to happen, the ones who continued to struggle even when Madonna was on to her next success" (n.p.).

Example 1: When Kayla Lewis was 19 years old, she made a Vine video in which she used the phrase "eyebrows on fleek." The video quickly went viral with over 50 million loops (before Vine shut down) and over three million views on YouTube. Before long, companies such as Denny's, Forever 21, Taco Bell, and IHOP had all used the phrase "on fleek" in marketing campaigns (Roth-Gordon et al., 2020, p. 108), never crediting Kayla Lewis (much less paying her for her creative content). Kayla's experience is a specific example of a common phenomenon: corporations using linguistic creativity[5] originating within the Black community for their own profit without credit or compensation.[6]

Example 2: One of the threats of linguistic appropriation is misuse and misinterpretation, and Coca-Cola gives us a perfect example. In 2018, Coke launched a marketing campaign in New Zealand that used the slogan "Kia Ora, Mate," an attempt to combine the Indigenous language of Māori with the colloquial term "mate" (meaning "friend"); however, while "kia ora" means "hello" in Māori, "mate" means "death" (Meixler, 2018). While an embarrassing gaffe for the company, this episode speaks to a broader blind spot—clearly no one from Coke thought it worthwhile or important enough to consult advisors from the culture they were attempting to use in their marketing.

Example 3: Although rapper-singer Iggy Azalea is White and doesn't speak Black Language in public spaces, she raps using features of Black Language in an attempt to align herself with hip hop culture. In 2015, Eberhardt and Freeman analyzed all of Azalea's current albums along with interviews. They found that in her albums, she uses the zero copula,[7] a grammatical structure of Black Language, 75% of the time in her songs but close to 0% in her interviews (2015, p. 315). Does being White mean that rap is off-limits to an artist as a genre? What about the Beastie Boys and Eminem? Well, as Eberhardt and Freeman (2015) point out, these White artists didn't use Black Language as a vehicle for their own profit. The Beastie Boys "rapped with high-pitched, nasal voices readily identified as white" (p. 307), and Eminem names his privileged position as a White man in hip hop throughout his lyrics (p. 308). In the same study of the zero copula cited above, Eminem uses them less than 15% of the time in his lyrics (p. 315).[8]

Since money and the idea of "legal rights" can easily be involved in discussions of linguistic and cultural appropriation, even lawyers have definitions of this concept. Susan Scafidi, a law professor at Fordham University and the author of *Who Owns*

---

5. "Fleek" was already used when Kayla made her video; however, "on fleek" uses the grammatical structure "on point" to emphasize how good her eyebrows looked (Roth-Gordon et al., 2020).

6. And there are even bigger issues beyond credit and compensation, which we will get to shortly.

7. This is a linguistic term, also known as the copula absence (Rickford, 1999), that describes a grammatical construction in Black Language wherein the "to be" construction is understood as in "You funny" or "She happy." Note that this construction can only happen with "is" or "are" (not "am"), and can only occur with the subject, so "That where they are" works but not "That is where they."

8. We can see an interesting conversation here in the classroom about modern White rappers, such as Post Malone and Jack Harlow.

Culture? Appropriation and Authenticity in American Law defines cultural appropriation as:

> Taking intellectual property, traditional knowledge, culture expressions, or artifacts from someone else's culture without permission. This can include unauthorized use of another culture's dance, dress, music, language, folklore, cuisine, traditional medicine, religious symbols, etc. It is most likely to be harmful when the source community is a minority group that has been oppressed or exploited in other ways or when the object of appropriation is particularly sensitive, e.g., sacred objects.
>
> (n.p.)[9]

However, this definition doesn't include an important point we have to consider: when cultural artifacts (particularly language) are used in new spaces, a double standard often emerges. As we have seen in the examples throughout this section, companies are happy to use and profit from phrases like "oh, snap" and "on fleek"; however, those same companies expect that such language is used solely for advertising and never in an interview. Likewise, many folks use slang which originated within the Black community, but consistently label Black Language (the language that gave them that slang) as wrong or inappropriate or bad (especially in spaces such as school). This linguistic double standard is one of the most problematic aspects of linguistic appropriation, and one that should be brought to the forefront of any discussion.

THE COMPLICATIONS OF LINGUISTIC AND CULTURAL APPROPRIATION

In the section below, we offer a framework for exploring linguistic and cultural appropriation with your students; however, here we would like to embrace what a slippery subject this is. Like many terms in the political landscape, linguistic and cultural appropriation lives in cultural contexts, political contexts, power contexts, and economic contexts (to name just a few), ultimately meaning that it is a difficult term to always use fairly and appropriately.

For example, in the June 2021 "Human Interest" section of *Slate*, a White parent writes about his concern that his child is being forced to learn Spanish at school:

> I do not think white people should speak Spanish as it is cultural appropriation in my eyes. Latinx people have been mocked for speaking Spanish, and to congratulate a white child for learning it and speaking it doesn't sit well with me.
>
> (Richards, 2021)

The *Slate* respondent, Doyin Richards, offers an important note that can help us differentiate between what is and is not appropriation; he says, "It's not like [the child's] mocking Latin culture by running around with a sombrero yelling, 'Arriba! Andale!' like Speedy Gonzales. He's simply learning a language that is commonly used across America" (Richards, 2021).

---

9. Cited in Baker (2012): https://jezebel.com/a-much-needed-primer-on-cultural-appropriation-30768539.

While this example may seem an extreme of misunderstanding linguistic appropriation, the line around linguistic and cultural appropriation isn't always as clear. For example, where are the boundaries (if any) around the following examples?

- Eating food outside of your culture
- Making food outside of your culture
- Becoming a chef of food outside of your culture and then profiting off teaching people, for example, how to correctly use chopsticks (even if you didn't grow up using chopsticks)

And beyond those examples, we must further consider how different cultural artifacts might have different measures of appropriation. For example, are there different levels of appropriation? Is enjoying a meal from another culture the same as using another culture's religious artifacts?[10] And when it comes to language, what's the difference between language change and linguistic appropriation? What's the difference between a speaker accommodating another speaker by using features of their dialect or language when communicating with them versus "appropriating" those features?

So many of the answers to these questions are embedded in other questions. Who's benefiting? Who's given credit? What's the intention? And, importantly, is there a double standard (as in the linguistic appropriation discussion above)? Do you love the jewelry/clothes/language/food of certain cultures—but disdain (or at least not advocate for) the people associated with the culture from which it comes? Below, we offer a framework and a project idea to explore these questions with your students; however, even the framework doesn't provide clear-cut answers. As we said above, when concepts are embedded in culture, power, politics, and economics, we are in for an interesting and important ride.

WHAT DOES THIS LOOK LIKE IN A CLASSROOM?

So now let's get onto the "how" of teaching linguistic and cultural appropriation in the classroom. First, share with students some of the examples we discussed earlier, or go out in the digital world and find your own—the internet is rife with them. Use the framework below to lead a discussion around whether the example is cultural or linguistic appropriation. Remember that there are few easy examples of linguistic and cultural appropriation; the ones we offered earlier in this section are about as close as you can get. Despite this, we encourage students to question everything—questions mean thinking, and we like that—so allow students to really grapple with the examples and framework. Throughout these discussions with our students, we also stay attuned to resistance. We think there is *good resistance*, which often comes in the form of critical questions, and *bad resistance*, which might happen because students are uncomfortable with questioning practices in which they themselves participate. We want to fully own here that these are tough conversations. But just because they are tough conversations doesn't mean that we shouldn't have them.

---

10. We know the answer to this one: No. Don't use other culture's religious artifacts. However, just because we feel pretty confident about this answer doesn't mean it isn't worth posing to your students.

Framework for Discussion (Based on Tran, 2016)

1. First, ask students to identify what ethnic/racial/cultural group created the chosen artifact or practice.

    - Take a minute to look it up, noting that it won't take long (and we agree). Honestly, it may be difficult to find the answer, particularly if students are looking up a specific slang phrase. If this is the case, you may encourage them to expand their research to question where most American slang originates.

2. Once students know where the practice or artifact originated, ask students to research the group's history and experiences around oppression.

    - Hop onto Wikipedia to find this out. If they followed step one and found the group to whom the practice or artifact belongs, they should go to that group's Wikipedia page. If they find words such as *slavery, colonialism,* or *genocide* on the page, Tran says take a moment and consider larger implications of using the artifact or practice "because a huge part of cultural appropriation is how historical patterns replay themselves in the current day" (n.p.).

3. Students should ask themselves if they benefit from doing this? How?

    - History matters (see #2 above): "What does it look like when someone thinks the art [or clothes or hairstyles or language of a particular culture] are cool, but not the people with whom it originates" (n.p.)?[11]

4. Ask students if the use of the artifact or practice would make someone from the originating group uncomfortable.

    - Here, we need some empathy—some attempt at understanding someone else's perspective. (We are going to talk more about empathy below.) Let's say someone takes up a part of your culture, benefits from it, profits off of it, but doesn't really care or advocate for your culture writ large, would you be upset? Yeah. You would. And so would we.

5. Encourage students to consider what makes it possible for them to engage with this practice, tradition, or material?

    - Has someone in the originating culture invited them to engage? What is their personal history with the culture or artifact? To help students grapple with this question, you may ask them to read the article "When Is It Okay to Wear the Clothing of Another Culture?" by Malaka Gharib (see Gharib, 2018) in which the author explores the blurry and moving lines between appreciation and appropriation.

A Moment with Critical Empathy

In Step 4 above, we (and Tran, 2016) use the word "empathy," which is one of those words that's thrown around a lot these days. We want to take a moment here and dig

---

[11]. We will get into this double standard (I like *the thing* but I don't like *the thing with the people who created it*) later in this section. It is an important part of appropriation and one we need to continue questioning.

into that word, exploring how "empathy" is commonly defined. Then, we'll share a possible revision on "empathy."

When a lot of us think of empathy, we might think of To Kill a Mockingbird (Lee, 1982) and that all important moment when Atticus tells Scout that you don't really know a man until you get in his skin and crawl around, a distinctly American Southern interpretation of "walking a mile in another man's shoes." This feels easy. Consider another person's perspective. Cool. Done. However, this type of empathy simplifies some pretty important aspects like history and culture. Being empathetic isn't just about considering someone else's point of view. That just makes for, maybe, a nicer world but not a better world.

So what does it mean to truly be empathetic?

Rather than considering empathy as, "yeah, I'm going to consider your perspective and BAM! I'm empathetic," what if we considered *empathy as translation* (see Pedwell, 2016)? Let's break this down a little. When someone translates a work from one language to another, it isn't enough to merely translate the words. (This would be the easy empathy talked about earlier, the Atticus Adage.) If you just translate the words in a text, you're missing out on the important stuff. A good translator considers the social, political, and historical context of the work in order to create a fair translation. This is a *critical* translation, honoring the context of the words, not simply the words themselves. Likewise, Pedwell urges us to move toward *critical* empathy, one that honors the social, political, and historical context of experiences. This critical empathy is a perfect partner for questioning linguistic and cultural appropriation because it is the complications (and the ignoring of the complications) around social, political, and historical contexts that often makes appropriation (instead of appreciation).

CULTURAL AND LINGUISTIC APPROPRIATION: LOOKING OUT

After providing space to discuss the definitions and complications of linguistic and cultural appropriation within a frame of critical empathy, it is time to set students free into the digital landscape. We think for this first foray into analysis, group work is best. First, ask students to identify a possible example of linguistic and/or cultural appropriation in the digital worlds in which they live. Then, have them analyze the example applying Tran's framework (2016). They will need to come to a conclusion: Is their example linguistic/cultural appropriation or not? They will need to justify their conclusion using Tran's framework as a guide. They can present their research in any number of digital spaces, but the center of the assignment should be questioning the presence of linguistic and cultural appropriation in the everyday digital landscape.

CULTURAL AND LINGUISTIC APPROPRIATION: LOOKING IN

A key component to social justice is bringing learned information out into the world with the goal of making the world a more just and equitable place for all people (which is hopefully what students will do by "looking out" as discussed above). However, we also need to have a conversation with students about the threats of identifying linguistic and cultural appropriation within our digital call-out culture—where social justice sometimes equates to berating people online. This isn't real social justice. We think a discussion about impact is important here. Which has more impact? Calling out folks online or having critical conversations about linguistic and cultural appropriation with those around us and *even with ourselves*?

Let us explain what we mean: We think students should question their own practices with Tran's framework above. It is easy to point the finger at someone else. It is hard to look at ourselves with the same lens. However, after following the steps we discussed above, we encourage you to create a space where your students question their own practices for potential examples of cultural and linguistic appropriation.

CONCLUSION

We know linguistic and cultural appropriation can be difficult to nail down, but we also have no question that it exists. It is an important part of our modern conversations around culture and power in digital spaces, and one we believe worth bringing into the classroom.

REFERENCES

Asmelash, L. (2021, July 2). Black creators wouldn't dance on TikTok to the latest Megan Thee Stallion track. Here's why their strike matters. *CNN Entertainment*. https://www.cnn.com/2021/07/02/entertainment/black-tiktok-strike-trnd/index.html

Baker, K. J. M. (2012, November 13). A much-needed primer on cultural appropriation. *Jezebel*. https://jezebel.com/a-much-needed-primer-on-cultural-appropriation-30768539

Dimen-Schein, M. (1977). *The anthropological imagination*. McGraw-Hill.

Eberhardt, M., & Freeman, K. (2015). "First things first, I'm the realest": Linguistic appropriation, white privilege, and the hip-hop personality of Iggy Azalea. *Journal of Sociolinguistics*, *19*(3), 303–327. https://doi.org/10.1111/josl.12128

Garvey, M. (2021, April 6). Jimmy Fallon responds to backlash over Addison Rae TikTok dance segment. *CNN Entertainment*. https://www.cnn.com/2021/04/06/entertainment/jimmy-fallon-addison-raes-tiktok/index.html

Gharib, M. (2018, October 26). When is it okay to wear the clothing of another culture? *NPR*. https://www.npr.org/sections/goatsandsoda/2018/10/26/658924715/when-is-it-ok-to-wear-the-clothing-of-another-culture

Hirsch, F. (2017, May 14). Is this the year advertisers wake up to perils of cultural appropriation? *The Guardian*. https://www.theguardian.com/media/2017/may/14/is-this-the-year-advertisers-wake-up-to-perils-of-cultural-appropriation

Lee, H. (1982). *To kill a mockingbird*. Warner Books.

Meixler, E. (2018, October 16). Coco-Cola's attempt to use New Zealand's indigenous Māori language misfires. *Time*. https://time.com/5425550/coca-cola-new-zealand-maori-hello-death/

Online Etymology Dictionary. (n.d.) *Appropriation*. Retrieved August 18, 2021. https://www.etymonline.com/word/appropriation

Pedwell, C. (2016). De-colonising empathy: Thinking affect transnationally. *Samyukta: A Journal of Women's Studies*, *16*(1), 27–49.

Richards, D. (June 29, 2021). Care and feeding: No to Spanish. Slate. https://slate.com/human-interest/2021/06/maximizing-sleep-with-infants-parenting-advice-from-care-and-feeding.html

Rickford, J. R. (1999). *African American vernacular English*. Blackwell Publishers.

Roth-Gordon, J., Harris, J., & Zamora, S. (2020). Producing white comfort through "corporate cool": Linguistic appropriation, social media, and @BrandsSayingBae. *International Journal of the Sociology of Language*, *2020*(265), 107–128. https://doi.org/10.1515/ijsl-2020-2105

Saveriano, M. (2020). The complicated case of Madonna's "Vogue." *Fansided*. https://fansided.com/2020/03/27/madonna-vogue-cultural-appropriation-question/

Tran, K. (2016, May 2). 5 simple questions that'll help you avoid unintentional cultural appropriation. *Everyday Feminism*. https://everydayfeminism.com/2016/05/avoid-cultural-appropriation/

INDEX

Note: Italicized page numbers refer to figures, **bold** page numbers refer to tables and page numbers followed by n refer to footnote.

academic disciplines 6
academic English 25
accent 8
account 17, **53**, **56**, 66–67, 81, 87, 92–95, 95n6, 99, 105
acronyms 8, **8**
activity 27–28, 27n8, 34–35, 37, 39–41, 45–46, 48, 50, 53, 65, 71, 102
adjective 34–35, 35n20, **39**, 42–46, **43**, 43n7, **44**, **46**, 53–56, 54n39, **54**, *55*, **56**, 82; *see also* clauses
adolescents 4, 10–11, 16
adverb 32n14, 32n18, 34, 35n20, 43, **43**, 45–46, **46**, 105; *see also* clauses
advertisements 17, 67, 75, 94
advertising 44, 67, 68, 70, 75–76, 81, 97, 100, 102n15, 112
affordances 3, 26, **36**, 37, 53, 58, 69, 72, 74, 80, 91, 93, 96–97, 102n15; *see also* digital
alliteration 84
amplification 43, **43**, 100
animation 34–36, **36**
appropriation cultural 15, 74, 74n8, 92, 109, 110n4, 111–116; linguistic 15, 74n8, 92, 109–116, 110n2
art 8, *39*, 114
article news 6, 15n4, 80n14, 81, 114; part of speech 34–35, 35n20
assignment 39–40, 72, 102, 115
audience 3, 17, 39, 43, 68, 75–76, 83–85, 93–94, 97, 98n11, 100–102, 102n14
authenticity 15–16, 93–95, 100, 112

bias 24, 48, 84, 87
Black 15, 23, 74, 74n7, 83, 110–112, 111n7

blackpill 14
blending 8, **8**
business 67, 93, 98, 107

Canva 55, **56**, 65, 102, 105
cardboard 44–46, *45*, **46**, 105; *see also* digital tools, Google cardboard
celebrity 92–95, 100
challenges vi, 4, 97–102
change 6, 18, 24, 27–29, 38, 40, 42, 69, 85, 91–93, 101–103, 103n16, 107, 110, 113
channels 68, 76, 80, 85n21, 93, 96
character 26n6, 51, 54, 72, 99–101
checklists 17–18; 68
classes: closed 34; open 34; teaching 7
classroom i, 6, 14n2, 15–18, 25–26, 34, 37, 44n29, 49n34, 59–60, 71–73, 87, 92, 101–103, 107, 110n4, 111n8, 113, 116; English language arts (ELA) 3, 15, 26–27, 72, 86, 102; Facebook 37; focus 25; university 8, 27; use 68
clauses 28, 31–34, **32**, **34** 51–52, 51, 57–59, 57, 60n49; adjectival 32n14; adverbial 32n14; dependent 31–34, **32**, **34** 32n15, 57, 60n49; independent 31–34, 32n18, **32**, **34**, **51**, 51–52, **57**, 57–59
clipping 8, **8**
code-switching 8
codes 25, 66
collective agreements 10
colons 50–53, **51**, **53**, 99; *see also* punctuation
color 8, 36, 98; people of (POC) 74, 110n4
combining 40n24, **42**, 55, 71–72
comma 11, 11n10, 26, **51**, 56–60, **57**, 57n40, 57n41, 59n45, 59n47, **60**; misplaced

24, 56; Oxford 23, 57n40; splice 57–58, 59n46, 75; *see also* punctuation
commentary 11, 32, 34, 41, 58n44, 84n20
communication 3–4, 7, 13, 23, 26, 29, 31, 33, 37, 50, 53, 58n43, 68, 74, 82, 101; elliptical 11
communicative modes 7
communities 13–14, 70, 91, 95, 102
competition 65, 100
composing 72, 75
conjunction 34, 36–38, 37n21, **38, 51,** 57, 58; coordinating 38
connectivity 69, 76
conspiracy theories 70, 79–80, 86, 95–96
constraints 26, 35, 52–53, 58, 74, 82, 92, 95, 102n15
context 3, 7, 8n8, 10–11, 15, 17, 23, 25–28, 34–35, 43–44, **43**, 53, 58–60, 72–73, 75, 82, 92, 94, 96–102, 115
convergence 69
copying 71–72
corporations 15–16, 18, 67, 95, 111
creativity 7–8, 11–12, 37, 55, 65–66, 70–72, 110–111
creators 23, 36, 47, 66, 69–70, 73, 83, 102, 110n3
credibility 16, 18, 24, 96, 100
critical lens 17
Critical Race Theory (CRT) 83
critical readers 18, 36
critical translation 115
cultural appreciation 110
cultural artifacts 112–113
cultural ethnographers 74
cultural exchange 110
cultural form 14
cultural influence 65
cultural investigator 75
culture: African 110; American 95; call-out 115; cancel 85, 85n22; club 110; consumer 75; definition 109; educational 72; empathy 115; ethnography 75, 76n9; expressions 112; food 113; hip hop 111; Latin 112; modern 58; multimodal remix 72; online media 28; originating 114; participatory digital 69; popular 29, 73; power 116; religious artifacts 113; shifts 3; sociological aspects 13, 15; subculture 5; youth 5; *see also* cultural appropriation
curriculum 25, 91, 91n1

data 67, 67n6, 72
declaratives 27n8, 28n9, 28n11, 80
delinquency 5
democracy 14, 18, 69, 96
dialect **8,** 25
digital: advertising 75; affordances 72, 80; blackface 74; consumer 17, 76; consumerism 17; creation 17, 66n2; ecosystem 66; environment 13, 65; expression 23; grammar 3–4; memes 28–29, 73; propaganda 68; reading 5; scrapbooks 53, 55–56, **55, 56**; space 3, 7–8, 11–17, 21, 24–25, 27, 35, 37–38, 57, 63, 65–66, 72, 75–76, 92, 115–116; tools i, 3–4, 24–26, 39, 60, 65–66, 71–72, 101–102, 107; video 76; world i, vi, 4, 7, 16, 18, 26, 65, 113, 115
digital tools: Adobe Spark 39, 55, 102; Amazon 44, 67n6; Anchor 49; Audacity 49; Canva 55, 65, 102, 105; Crello 55; DesignBold 55; FlipGrid 49, 107; Flipsnack 39; GoAnimate 35; Google 34, 44, 67, 105; Google Arts and Culture 44; Google Cardboard 44–46, **45, 46**; Google Doc 104; Google Jamboard 27–28, **28**, 29, 102, 104; Google Slides 39, **42**; Linoit.it 27; Mematic 34; Memedroid 34; Memefactory 34; Pear Deck 39; Photoshop 65n1; PowerPoint 39, **42**; Powtoon 35; Sites in VR 44; Soundtrap 49; Spotify 49; Toontastic 35; VoiceThread 39, **42**; Within VR 44, **46**; YouCut 60, 69; *see also* digital
directed practice 72
disinformation 18, 86–87, 92, 95–97, 96n8; *see also* information

echo chambers 14
education 13, 16–18, 35, 68, 91
emoji 5, 7, 49
emoticons 7–8, **8,** 50–51, **51**
empathy 114–115
engagement 65–66, 69
English: classroom 3, 15, 26, 48, 86; language 5–8, 10–11, 24–26, 50, 57n42, 59, 69, 71, 102, 109, 110n2; standardized 11, 50, 57, 57n41, 59; teachers 4, 10, 36, **39**, 56, 75, 84, 93n3; *see also* academic English; Standard American English
English Language Arts (ELA) 3, 24, 26, 36, 69, 71, 86, 91
enregisterment 14
environmental justice 103
equity 86, 91–92, 104
ethnographic stance 75
ethnography 75, 76n9
etymology 109
evolution 6–7, 12, 69, 75

experiences 33, 45, 65, 71, 75, 95, 101, 114–115
experimentation 37, 65–66, 100

Facebook 23–24, 36–38, 67, 75, 102, 102n14, 105; *see also* social media platforms
failure 66, 107
fake news 87
floating signifiers 33
fluency 18, 37, 43, 69
food 16, **51**, 69, 92, 97–98, 98n11, 103–104, 109, 113
format 26, 73, 107
fragments 28, 75, 99

game 5, 18, 35–36, **36**, **43**, 65–66, 66n3, 69, 75; game-based entertainment 65; gamification 65; gaming 36, 65, 66n2; *see also* video gaming
generalization 83–84, 93, 95
generalizing 83
generation 4, 102
genre 24, 27n7, 31, 37, 74–75, 80, 93, 99–100, 100n12, 111
gestures 29, 58
grammar: applied i; bad/incorrect/violations 6, 10, 23; books 12, 28, 32n15, 35n20, 39; brushstrokes 44; classes 7, 26; concepts 25, 25n3, 31, 39, 54, 58n43, 59–60, 97; digital 3–4; exercises 26; implicit 58; instruction 24, 26, 34, 37, 47, 57, 60, 91; memes 80; performance 11; relevance 87; remix 73, 75–76; rhetorical i, 25–26, 37, 60; task 11; tests 10; use 93; worksheets 17
graphic digital design 65
graphics 66, 72, 75, 99
group belonging 15n4; far-left 86; in-group 14–15, 37, 96; members/membership 15, 23, **36**; minority 112, 114; out-group 14, 37, 96; protestors 77; researchers 10–11; right-leaning 14; special interest 18, 75; terrorist 80; work 40, **42**, 48, **50**, 81–82, 102–105, 104n17, 107, 114–115; *see also* status

hashtag 11, **53**, 75, 94, 105
hedging 47, 49, 83–84
high school 4, 10, 17, 23, **39**, 45, 53, 56, 71
history 3, 7–8, 7n6, 10, 11n10, 12–13, 16, 34, **43**, 52, 68, 70, 109, 109n1, 114–115
homophones 8
human connection 17
humor 30–34, **34**, 40, 58, 73, 82
hyphens 53–54, 99

identity 13, 15–16, 37, 37n22, 53, 55–56, **56**, 57n40, 68, 72, 74, 92, 94, 100–101
identity markers 16, 101
ideology/ideologies 14
idiom 29
imagery 8, 74–75, 98–99
images 14, 27, 33, 37, 39–42, **42**, 44–46, **46**, 54–56, **55**, 74, 76, 93–94, 99, 103, 105, 107
imperatives 27n8, 28n9, 80, 82, 85
improvisation 66
inequity 13
influence 4, 5, 17, 24, 65
influencers 35, **36**, 76, 93
information 8, 14–15, 17–18, 24, 29, 36, 40n25, 49–51; **50**, **51**, 58, 67–70, 72, 76, 79–80, 83, 96–97, 99, 107, 115; *see also* disinformation; information ecosystem; silos of information
information ecosystem 24, 72
initialism 8, 8
Instagram 24, 26n6, 36–38, **38**, 67, 69, 72, 76, 93–94, 102, 105, 107
institutions 13–14
integration 25
interactions 3, 44, 76
interests 6, 69, 71, 71n1, 80, 86n24, 91–93, 100
internet 5–8, 7n6, 13–15, 18, 23, **28**, **34**, **36**, **38**, **42**, **50**, **56**, 67–70, 67n4, 73, 86, 95–96, 101–105, 113
internet language i, 6
irony 31, 34, **34**, 58, 73

landscape 5–6, 13, 46, 65, 84, 91, 112, 115
language: -based 6; Black 15, 111–112, 111n7; change 7, 110, 113; ELA 3, 24, 26, 36, 69, 71, 86, 91; experts with 25; foreign 25; internet i, 6; meme 5; resources 7; standard 6, 10; study 24–25, 35, 49n34, 60, 87; variation 14
Latinx 110, 112
learning 3, 33, 65–67, 72, 91, 102
legacy media 69
legitimacy 58, 83
lesson 16–18, 25n4, 26
lexical categories 34, 36, **36**
LGBTQ 110, 110n4
lifestyle 94
linguistic patterns 31
linguistics 3, 7, 7n6, 12
literacy: conventional 5; critical 16; critical digital i, 16–17, 75, 91; critical memetic 73; definition 26; digital 3, 13, 16–17, 34,

INDEX **119**

71; emergent 24; media 33, 68; power and language 87; skills 10; standards 5; technology and 4
loan words 110

mainstream 11, 15, 24, 49, 69, 74, 81, 96
marketing 16, 58, 75, 98–99, 111
mechanics 7, 10–11, 59n46
media: Common Sense 13, 16; corporate 78; digital i, 17, 24, 58, 95, 107; legacy 69; literacy 33, 68; mainstream 49, 69; mass 99–100; online media culture 28; social 3, 10, 14, 17, 24, 34, 36–38, **38**, 49, 52, 54, 67–68, 68n7, 70, 76, 80–82, 84, 86–87, 92–97, 95n6, 101–102, 102n14, 102n15, 105, 107
Media Manipulation Casebook 96
meme: analysis 31; Bad Luck Brian 30, *30*; communication 74, 82; creation 31, 34, **34**, 97, 105; culture 73; definition 28–29; clauses 32–33; digital 28–29, 73; discussion 59; disinformation 86; generator 34, **34**; grammar 80; Hey Girl 30–31, *31*; humor 31, 58n44; image 33, 37; internet 73; language 5; One Does Not Simply 30, *31*; politics 68–69; rhetorical use 73–74, *73*; Success Kid 29, *29*; text 32n18, 33; When You Realize 32, *32*
mentor texts 27, 54
messages 8, 11, 23–24, 29, 52, 59, 67, 93, 104
meta-commentary 11
meta-knowledge 11
metaphors 28, 59–60
middle school 17
mobile device 34, 37, **53**, 69, 76
mode 7, 26, 39, 59–60, 68
modeling 72
modern propaganda education 68
mood 94
moral panic 5–6
movement 8, 23, 33, 67
multimodality 91
music 49, 65, 66n2, 93, 110, 112
MySpace 26

narrative 16, 27n7, 40, **42**, 55, 86–87, 89, 92, 96, 98n11, 100
National Writing Project 92, 92n2, 102
National Council of Teachers of English (NCTE) 26
native speaker 25
norms 69, 96
noun: classes 34–35, 34n19; definition 27, 35–36, **36**; function 35–36, 35n20, **36**; hyphenated 53–56, **54**, 54n39, **56**; implications 79; phrases **39**, **44**, 44n31

omission **8**, 10, 77
online affordances 3; attention 75; availability 37; call-out culture 115–116; community 37, 37n22, 96; consumers 70; content 70n8, 86; critical readers 18; disinformation 17–18, 83, 92; experiences 95; gaffes 23; games 36; identity 15, 37, 37n22; information 17; marketing 58; media culture 28; meme generators 34, **34**; platform 97; players 69; post 24, 37; presence 36; spaces 3, 13, 15–16, 23, 72, 84; spelling 8; time 8, 16–17; use 11; website 24; worlds 35–36, **36**; *see also* digital
opportunities 4, 34, 66, 76, 92
optimal experience 65
orthography 8, **8**

parallelism 31, 31n13
pause marking 11
perception 97
persona 93–95, 99–101
perspective: adaptation 6; critical 3; ethnographic 75–76; fresh 46; gain 59; grammatical 75; linguistic 25; particular 44–45, 47, 75, 94, 114–115; pedagogical 5, 33–34, 72
phonetics/phonetic 8
Photoshop 65n1; *see also* digital tools
phrase: absolute 38–42, *39*, *41*, **42**; adjectival 42–47, **43**, **44**, 44n31, **46–47**, 99; alliteration 85; appropriation and 111–112; be played 66; clauses 32; descriptive 54; humorous 58n44; ideological 109; initialism 8; memes 29, 31; nonsentence 27; noun 44n31; participial 38–42, *39*, *40*, **42**; slang 15, 114; within sentences 28
pictorial imagery 8
play 8–9, 11, 24, 27, 34n19, 65–67, 67n4, 85n21, 102n15
podcasts 47–50, *49*, *50*
posts 10–11, 23–24, 27, 36–38, **38**, 76, 93–94, 97, 103, 107
power: colons 52; concepts 113; condensation symbol 85; consumer 67; contexts 112; creative 55, 102; critical digital literacy 16; dialects 25; digital video 76; digital spaces 116; identity 13–16, 68, 92; language 13–14, 26, 79, 84, 87; memetic communication 74; nouns 35; online 13–14; phrases 44; propoganda 68; shifts

48; silos of information 14; structures 13–14; voice 47
preservice teachers i, 26–27
privacy 37, 67, 95
privilege 25, 72, 111
process 14, 35, 58, **60**, 71, 79, 92, 92, 99, 101–102, 104, 107
profile 67, 72, 94
projects 91–93, 102, 107
propaganda 14, 17, 24, 52, 68–70, 86, 94
propagation 68
public discourse 6
punctuation: colon/semicolon 50–53, **51**; comma 56–57, 57n41, 59; creative 23, 75; mechanics 11; syntactic 11; typographical 11
purpose 11, 25, 31, **34**, 36, 41–44, **43**, 53, 54n39, 80, 86, 91, 107

questions 4, 15–17, 28, 35, **36**, 37, 68, 73–75, 77–79, 82–85, 92–94, 103, 107, 113

reading 3, 5–8, 7n5, 14, 17–18, 24, 34, 36, 85
reciprocal teaching 35
reduplication **8**
remix 55, 58, 71–74
representation 14–15, 55, 74, 74n7, 77, 99
research 6, 8, 10–11, 13, 17, 24, 34, 48, 58, 72, 77, 84, 96, 97n10, 98, 104, 107, 114–115
resistance 113
rhetoric 24n2, 76, 85, 91, 93, 102, 107; rhetorical grammar i, 21, 25–26, 37, 60; rhetorical situation 25, 37

school 4, 8, 10, 17, 23, 37, 45, 48, 53, 56, 68, 71–72, 81, 91n1, 92, 105, 112
secondary ELA 27
secondary students 27
semicolons 50–53, **51**, 52, **53**, 56, 57; *see also* punctuation
semiotic/semiotics 8
sentence: clauses **32**, 32n15; colon/semicolon 50–53, **51**, 52n36, **53**; combining 40, **42**; commas 56–60, **57**, 57n41, 59n45, **60**, 60n49; complete 11, 27, 39; complex 32; conjunctions 38, **38**; construction 27; creation 27; definition 27; elliptical 10–11; form 82, 99; fragment 75, 99; hedging 83; hyphenated adjectives **56**; image 40, **42**, 42n26; language of 25; level 10; mentor 27, **28**; modifier 59; nonsentence 27, **28**, 32, 32n15, 32n16; phrases **39**, 40, **44**; questions about 77; rhetorical choice 37;

structure 27, 75, 82; tense/voice 47, **47–48**; types 27n8, 28, 28n9, 29n11; *see also* grammar, punctuation
silos of information 14
simplistic binaries 81–82, 82n16
slang 15, 112, 114; *see also* appropriation
slogan 77, 84–87, 98, 105, 111
Snapchat 37, 102
social: action 91–92, 92, 101–102; change 24, 91–92; cohesion 95; contexts 13; identity 15; media 3, 10, 14, 17, 24, 34, 36–38, **38**, 49, 52, 54, 67–68, 68n7, 70, 76, 80–82, 84, 86–87, 92–97, 95n6, 101–102, 102n14, 102n15, 105, 107; network 72, 93, 95–96; panic 5; platform 17
social media platforms: Facebook 23–24, 36–38, 67, 75, 102, 102n14, 105; Instagram 24, 26n6, 36–37, **38**, 67, 69, 72, 76, 93–94, 102, 105, 107; TikTok i, 26n6, 37, 40, 56, 58, 60, **60**, 60n49, 67, 73, 75, 93, 107, 110; Twitter i, 11, 16–17, 24, 26n6, 50–53, **53**, 67, 81, 93, 102, 105; YouTube 40, 75, 93, 94n4, 107, 111
society 5, 13, 14, 16, 24, 70, 74, 91n1, 96
sociocultural theory 16
sociolinguistics 13
solutions 58, 101, 104–105, 107
spaces: classroom 71; digital 3–4, 7–8, 11–17, 21, 24–25, 27, 35, 37–38, 57, 63, 65–66, 72, 75–76, 92, 115–116; informal 8; linguistic 12; new 112; online 3, 13, 15–16, 23, 72, 84; open 37; particular 100; public 23, 111; real 12; school 112; sentence 27; social media 68, 93; standard language 6; standardized English 50; syntax 10; tools i, 3–4, 24–26, 39, 60, 65–66, 71–72, 101–102, 107; VR 44
spectrum 70, 76, 92
speech 10–11, 23, 27, 34, 77
spelling 6–8, **8**, 10, 23
spoken hashtags 11; *see also* hashtag
spoken punctuation 11
standard language 6, 10
Standard American English (SAE) 25
standardization 7–8, **8**
status: in-group 14–15, 37, 96; out-group 37, 96; quo 73, 99–100; resource 24; social media 36; socioeconomic 13
status marking 57–59, 59n47
stereotypes 53, 55, **56**, 74, 80, 83, 87, 93, 95, 99–100, 100n12
sticky notes 27–28, **28**, 29, 32n16
strategies i, 37, 47, 75, 87, 93

student: directions 28n10; discovery 93; -driven 107; groups 81–82, 104; handout 28, 34, 36, 38, 42, 46, 50, 53, 56, 60; knowledge 25; -led 92, 102; participants 18, 45, 49, 52, 57n40, 93; project 92; prose 53; strengths 6; tweet 52; understanding 59; work 56; writing 10, 58
symbols 9, 14–15, 85, 109, 112
synonyms 43, **43**
syntax 10, 66
synthetic personalization 15

tags 94
teachers 3–4, 7, 16–17, 24, 26, 34, 48, 56, 58, 79, 91, 93, 102, 104; English i, 4, 10, 36, 56, 75, 84; language arts 87; preservice i, 26–27; writing 92n2
technology i, 3–5, 25–26, 60, 65, 67, 69–70, 72–74, 76, 86, 91, 93, 95, 97, 101–102; *see also* digital
text: accompanying 40; alternate 33; -based 40; boxes 56; -centered 45; chunks of 40n23; choices **34**; combinations 28, *41*; complex 94; evolving 93; existing 58; feature **28**; future 59; images with 37–39, **38**, 41, *41*, **42**, 55, **56**; language 74, 86; meme 32–33, 32n18; mentor 27, 54; messages 8, 11; onscreen 39; original 10; propaganda 68; textisms 10; textspeak 6, 59; translate 115; written 56
theme 25, 107, 110
TikTok i, 26n6, 37, 40, 56, 58, 60, **60**, 60n49, 67, 73, 75, 93, 107, 110; *see also* social media platforms

tools: digital i, 3–4, 24–26, 39, 60, 65–66, 71–72, 101–102, 107; *see also* digital tools
transforming 55, 71–72
translation 115
Twitter i, 11, 16–17, 24, 26n6, 50–53, **53**, 60, 61, 67, 81, 88, 93, 102, 105; *see also* social media platforms
typography 7–8

ubiquity 76; ubiquitous connectivity 69
university i, 8, 93n3, 111
user-created tutorials 69, 75

varieties 14
verb 27, 29–30, **32**, 32, 34, **47–48**, **51**
vertical reading 18
video gaming 65
viral marketing 75
virtual reality 42, 44, *45*, **46**
voice: active **47**; competing 91; hedging 49; loud 69; passive 25, 47–50, **47**, 48n33, **50**; spoken 11, 14, 26, 78, 111

weaponization 86
website 17–18, 24, 26, 35, 37, 67, 71n2, 103, 105, 105n18, 107
White 74, 83, 110–112, 111n8
writing 3, 5, 7, 7n5, 10–11, 23, 25, **28**, 34, 34n19, 37, 45–47, 55–56, **56**, 58, 79n13, 91n1, 92n2; efficiency 9; instruction 24, 27n7

YouTube 40, 75, 93, 94n4, 107, 111; *see also* social media platforms

For Product Safety Concerns and Information please contact our EU representative GPSR@taylorandfrancis.com
Taylor & Francis Verlag GmbH, Kaufingerstraße 24, 80331 München, Germany

www.ingramcontent.com/pod-product-compliance
Lightning Source LLC
Chambersburg PA
CBHW060456300426
44113CB00016B/2613